Articles on Japanese Society, Economy, Management, Organization and Labor

'Maurie' Kaoru Kobayashi

JAPAN: THE MOST MISUNDERSTOOD COUNTRY

The **Japan Times**, Ltd.

ISBN4-7890-0247-0
Copyright © 1984 by 'Maurie' Kaoru Kobayashi
Jacket design by Atelier Hirata

First edition: July 1984
Third printing: February 1990

All rights reserved. No part of this book may be reproduced in any form without the permission of The Japan Times, Ltd.

Published by The Japan Times, Ltd.
5-4, Shibaura 4-chome, Minato-ku, Tokyo 108

Printed in Japan

Preface

As Japanese economy and business have expanded across the borders of the world and adeptly steered a course without striking the rocks despite postwar difficulties and two successive oil crises, world businessmen, politicians and scholars seem interested in exploring the secrets behind these "miraculous" Japanese maneuverings.

Triggered initially by the NBC series "If Japan can, why can't we?" which depicted painstaking Japanese means of quality assurance and the group-oriented decision-making system, the interest in probing the oriental mystique to account for the heretofore barely successful management of its economy has gained more momentum as books on Japan such as Ezra Vogel's *Japan as No. 1,* William Ouchi's *Theory Z,* and Athos Pascale's *The Japanese Management,* continue to pound the market.

This fever to learn more about Japanese business practices and management methods is still vivid in many countries, particularly in Europe and developing countries of late. The faddish American people, once attracted by the Japanese practice of business in the late '70s, have gone through the short love-hate syndrome with excessive emphasis and praise of excelling Japanese organizations. They seem to have reached the conclusion that excellent companies do share similar good management practices, be they American, Japanese or Singaporian. This kind of emphasis on identifying commonality rather than fancy differences is evident in an analysis made by Thomas J. Peters and Robert H. Waterman Jr.'s *In Search of Excellence* and *An Illu-*

sion — *Japan as No. 1* by Akira Ueno of the Nomura Research Institute. The interim report on comparative analysis of Japanese management published this year by the Japan Enterprise Overseas Association also supports this new commonality-directed approach.

However, during the past decade of the study of Japanese business and organization, many new misconceptions and misunderstandings have been born even among the most knowledgeable people about Japanese managerial practices. Before World War II, Fujiyama, samurai and the geisha girl were the symbols of old Japan. Kamikaze, Zero fighter, and Pearl Harbor became the reminders of Japan during the unhappy war. Sony, Honda, and Canon took the place of the prewar shoddy 'Made in Japan' products; now QC Circle, *nemawashi* and participative management are the three new image-provoking words of Japan.

As knowledge increases and more information is gathered with regard to the Japanese ways of doing business and managing people, stereotypes and obsolete models which describe the Japanese business world mushroom extensively.

For instance, the so-called three pillars of Japanese management institutions — the permanent employment system, seniority based wage system, and company union structure, are still widely accepted as constants in spite of the fact they are no longer valid descriptions of the actual Japanese management systems. These mistaken views are unfortunately burgeoning in many areas of business studies.

This book is solely designed to clear away some of the mist of misunderstanding and clarify the subtleties of some Japanese management techniques, and to contribute in a humble way to better international communicative efforts primarily in the business and management domains. Though I have written and edited close to three dozen books in Japanese, this is the first to be printed in English, and is an integration of my writings over the last ten years. Special care has been taken to update and revise the contents, to serve the readers' appreciation of the current state of the art in Japanese management and business administration.

My first thanks go to Dr. W. Warner Burke of Columbia University and Dr. Michael Cahn, who kindly accepted my request to reproduce their collaborative works with me. I would also like to thank the following organizations for allowing the reproduction of articles I wrote on previous occasions: Columbia Journal of World Business, English Economic Journal, The Wheel Extended of Toyota, News from Hotel Okura, Tradepia International of Nissho Iwai, and Japan Society of New York.

Last but not least my deepest appreciation must be expressed to two persons — Mr. Junichi Saito of The Japan Times and Ms. Michiko Yamamoto. Mr. Saito's constant encouragement and patience made this book possible, and Ms. Yamamoto's secretarial assistance made my dream to publish this first book in English come true.

'Maurie' Kaoru Kobayshi

June 1984

Table of Contents

Preface   iii

I

The Knowledge-Obsessed Japanese
Hidden Keys to the High-Performing Japanese Economy   3

The Aging and Affluent Nation   17

Organization Development in Japan
In Collaboration with W. Warner Burke   21

Productivity and Japanese Management Style
Interviewer: Meyer Michael Cahn, Ed. D.   43

Marketing in Japan: How to Sell in Japan Effectively   73

Japanese Management and Labor   89

Human Resources Development in Japan
Analysis of Its Wholistic Approach   94

Japan: Its Changing Life Style and Patterns   102

II

How to Do Business in Japan (1)
Joy and Agony of Learning Japanese   115

How to Do Business in Japan (2)
Study Denies 'Closed Japan' Concept; Shows Opportunities for Success   120

How to Do Business in Japan (3)
A Key to Doing Business with the Japanese: Tolerance for Ambiguity   125

How to Do Business in Japan (4)
Permanent Employment, Seniority Wage System, Enterprise Union Structure — Are All Simply Myths?   131

How to Do Business in Japan (5)
In Search of Excellent Japanese Companies   136

How to Do Business in Japan (6)
Ten Questions Most Frequently Asked Japanese Expatriates Working Abroad   141

How to Do Business in Japan (7)
Reading a Japanese like a Book Through the
Body Language   146

How to Do Business in Japan (8)
Toward Better Understanding of Sogo Shosha   151

How to Do Business in Japan (9)
Cashing In on the Changing Japanese Woman   156

How to Do Business in Japan (10)
The 'Time-Is-Short' Syndrome: Japan vs. the
U.S.   161

I

The Knowledge-Obsessed Japanese
Hidden Keys to the High-Performing Japanese Economy

The Information Explosion

Just after the end of World War II, Indian Prime Minister Jawaharlal Nehru reportedly told the ambassador from Japan, "There are three major requirements for becoming a full-fledged world power in the postwar era: a population of several hundred million, a vast territory, and natural resources." With these as the qualifications to be met, the possibility of becoming a world power would be limited to the United States, the Soviet Union, India, and China.

As evidenced by the rise of once war-devastated Japan and West Germany and the tiny, densely populated, resource-starved city-state of Singapore, however, history has shown the exact opposite to be true, thanks to their realization of tremendous economic growth, even though they are now suffering from the impact of the so-called "most serious postwar world synchronized recession."

I do not wish to be boastful about the miraculous recovery of Japan and her successful resilience in adjusting to two consecutive oil crises, but Japan is now actually the only country in the whole world that is able to maintain a "modest" economic growth rate of about 3 percent. Much study and analysis are required to accurately identify the secrets of the continuing Japanese economic "miracle."

In this article, however, let us confine our exploration to an often overlooked factor; that is, the thirst for information which characterizes the Japanese mentality as a key to explaining the high performance of the Japanese economy.

A person visiting Japan for the first time may be greatly surprised to observe — even before reaching his downtown Tokyo hotel after arriving at Narita International Airport — the sheer number and array of somewhat poorly organized, but hardly regulated advertising towers, billboards, notices and posters, carrying a variety of information. The stranger will be further surprised to learn that eight television channels plus a CATV network broadcast in fierce competition from 6 a.m. until late at night, almost twenty hours a day, while eleven FM, AM and shortwave radio stations entertain listeners almost around the clock. Four English-language newspapers compete desperately for readers. Circulation of each of the two major Japanese national newpapers (the *Asahi* and the *Yomiuri*) exceeds 7.5 million and circulations of five major national daily newspapers surpass 25 million.

Behind the hustle and bustle of the information wars, which sometimes result in over-communication and excessive exposure to the various mass media, the able observer will surely sense an insatiable thirst among the Japanese for information and knowledge.

Venturing into the streets, our visitor will find newsstands and bookstores on almost every corner in the major metropolitan areas, and even in remote small communities and rural areas. There he can choose from a variety of magazines and periodicals whose total circulation reaches 3.2 billion copies annually. Each year some 1.2 billion books are printed, a world record.

Dr. Iwao Nukata, an authority on information processing, estimates that the various media in Japan produce 2.3 quadrillion words each day, which translates to the equivalent of 200 billion paperbacks. And this information explosion never stops.

It is hardly surprising to learn, then, that two of the most popular words in the Japanese language are *joho* (information) and *chishiki* (knowledge). Dr. Fritze Machllup of Princeton University divides the knowledge industry into eight categories: education, research and development, publishing and printing, communication, information processing, information service, broadcasting, and entertainment. Japan has made enormous strides in all these categories. The knowledge industry already constitutes approximately 35 percent of the Gross National Product and employs nearly 55 percent of the workforce.

Like the Jewish mothers of legend, Japanese parents are obsessed with their children's education.

They spend more than 7 percent of their disposable income on education and learning. At the higher levels of education, 42.4 percent of Japanese males and 33.3 percent of the females go to college and other institutions of higher learning, exceeded only by their counterparts in the U.S.A. Nearly 94.3 percent of those who complete the nine years of compulsory education are enrolled in senior high schools for another three years of education. Thus two and a half million college and university students are studying at 1,036 colleges and universities. In terms of numbers, at any rate, this figure of 1,036 colleges and universities compares very well with the U.K.'s 78 and France's 71.

The Japanese communications industry has prospered by offering faddish Japanese consumers a variety of information-related equipment and gadgets. Thus the average household owns such consumer durables as color TV sets (in 98.9 percent of households), cameras (85.2 percent), tape recorders (64.7 percent), and videotape recorders (12 percent). So even the small rooms of the typical Japanese home are becoming "mini media rooms" equipped with all these modern communications facilities.

People in the fashion business now claim their industry should be included in the information-knowledge sector, since what they sell is actually "invisible information" about current fashions and brand names, in the form of apparel, furniture, and interior and home-furnishings. True enough, even a young lady working as a low-salaried office clerk purchases prestigious Louis Vuitton handbags and purses. College students like to boast of clothes that bear the status-symbol labels of Brooks Brothers and Burberry.

Cashing in on this craze and developing merchandizing campaigns for consumer products, Dentsu has become not only Japan's but the world's largest ad agency.

Television viewers can see Kirk Douglas, with his inimitable smile, as he speaks to them about Nestle's, or Prince Rudolf with his own cup of Nestle's President. In other commercial messages, Kojak grins wickedly at millions of innocent Japanese housewives who don't realize what he's really after, and Fara Faucet-Majors attracts the Japanese with her siren's smile.

Learn More to Earn More

Deluged by a barrage of information, Japanese business people are constantly reminded of the need to unlearn antiquated concepts and skills, and to acquire new knowledge by availing themselves of abundant educational opportunities. It is quite common for the young office worker, whose professional knowledge is said to be obsolescent every seven years, to attend personal-computer workshops, intensive business English courses, and public-speaking seminars. Almost all major Japanese companies offer many different subsidized courses to employees in such areas as robotics, computer science, effective management, international marketing, and business law, to name a few.

The incessant urge to update information is also seen in the business activities of Japanese companies themselves. Any one of the nine general trading firms (usually called sogo shosha), which dominate 49.5 percent of Japan's exports and 59.6 percent of her imports, sends and receives via telex tens of thousands of words of information each day. The quantity of information generated by one general trading company exceeds that handled daily by the country's Ministry of Foreign Affairs.

The information gathered and brought home by employees posted overseas is a further indication of Japanese business firms' overwhelming determination to absorb the most up-to-date information from the four corners of the earth. NEC companies, for example, send almost 8,000 employees abroad every year, Toshiba 6,000, Nippon Steel Corp. 5,500. The overseas staffs of the trading companies total 16,000 persons. JETRO, a government-supported organization whose purpose is to promote trade, now operates 75 offices around the world.

The patenting of new technology further reflects the search for the most sophisticated and advanced information. In 1980,

141,517 Japanese applicants filed for a total of 166,092 patents, while in the U.S. applicants numbered only 10,189 and applications 100,916, and France reported a mere 2,444 applicants and 37,137 applications.

Japan's Ministry of International Trade and Industry also plays a role in Japanese businesses' quest for information. Among its activities, for example, MITI supports WEIS (World Economic Information Service), which is designed to assist Japanese companies in obtaining current international business data. It also helps operate the Institute for International Studies, which, at its facilities located near Mt. Fuji, is mandated to train competent specialists in international trade and overseas management.

As another example of the government's acute awareness of the importance of both education and communications for the private sector in Japan, MITI's director of international business in the past five years has regularly assisted panels of experts in studying international communications problems.

Keen Intellectual Curiosity

Why are the Japanese so sensitive to the importance of information and knowledge in their pursuit of business activities? The answer lies in the historical, geographical, and cultural setting of Japan itself.

Defeated in battle and stripped of all colonial advantages by the terms of the surrender, the Japanese began searching their souls for ways in which to build a peaceful nation in the postwar period. They had to face the inescapable need to feed a hundred million starving people, plus the undeniable fact that their recovery would depend on a stabilized supply of natural resources from other countries.

Virtually the only resources we could claim for ourselves

were to be found under our hats. Japan's survival would depend on the use of our brains and a lively ingenuity. The scenario was, and still is in the main, to import natural resources from resource-rich countries, process them to add value and quality, and export such products to adequate markets. In order to achieve this goal, Japanese firms had to identify areas in which they could maximize this conversion process by first locating the most convenient and least costly raw materials, and then exploring the markets that would offer the greatest sales potential for their products. Thus did the postwar pilgrims among Japanese business people begin their attempt to acquire technology that would promise the greatest potential in terms of adaptation and application through careful, systematic analysis of the needs of consumers in different parts of the world.

It was a science article in Fortune magazine, for example, that in 1945 inspired the entrepreneurial spirit of two men, Masaru Ibuka and Akio Morita, to blaze new trials with an item called the transistor. In 1953, the Sony Corporation paid Western Electric ¥25,000 for the non-exclusive rights to manufacture transistors.

The Japan Productivity Center, meanwhile, organizes fifty overseas study teams each year to absorb the most advanced management techniques and thereby accelerate the emulation process of Japanese industries. These teams have so far numbered 1,470 and involved about 18,000 people.

It was our own Sanno Institute that pioneered the introduction of the behavioral science approach to optimize the utilization of human resources when we invited noted behavioral scientists and organizational development practitioners such as Frederick Herzburg, R.R. Blake and J.S. Mouton to come to Japan to disseminate their gospel for the more effective utilization of our manpower.

The great management guru Peter F. Drucker was invited to Japan more than ten times, and his erudite classic, *The Practice of Management,* has sold more than 2.8 million copies to date. This trend to absorb the hottest information from abroad is still viable and continues. Recent examples may be the almost simultaneous publications of non-fiction U.S. top-sellers like *Megatrends* by John Naisbitt and *The One Minute Manager* by Kenneth Blanchard and Spencer Johnson, which enjoy best-sellerdom in Japan, too.

Historical Perspective

Isolated geographically and historically from other parts of the world for nearly 300 years during the Tokugawa shogunate, Japan opened its doors to the world with the advent of the Meiji Restoration. At that time we Japanese showed great enthusiasm for catching up with Western civilization. But the hundred-year drive toward the modernization of Japan after the Meiji period can be traced back to even earlier times. Preceding this particular phase of modernization in the mid-19th century was a long history of the Japanese constantly being motivated and rewarded for learning more to earn more.

Japan's phenomenal industrial achievement is commonly attributed to its unique capacity for imitation. We Japanese have been called the world's leading copycats. There is no reason to be defensive about this accusation, since it was indeed an exceptional ability to emulate that lay — and continues to lie — behind the so-called copycat behavior of the Japanese. As Time magazine once reported, "Few nations have sought out and used the best from other societies as has Japan." In a sense Japan has become "the best of all possible worlds." To illustrate the point, I offer the example of the shipwrecked Portuguese mariners who went ashore on Tanegashima Island in 1543 and traded several firearms in exchange for food and water from the local inhabitants. For these Japanese it was the first encounter with Westerners and their weapons. Some 30 years later one of the Portuguese sailors happened to return to the same island, only to find to his great surprise that the people of the island were handsomely armed with some 20,000 "Tanegashima guns," each a precise replica of the original weapon.

The famous Confucian bible *Rongo* (The Analects of Confucius) begins with the well-known words, "What a joy to learn, and to put into practice what you have learned." This Confucian encouragement has been one of the major themes in Japanese education for a thousand years, helping pave the way for a ready acceptance of the importance of learning. In the postwar rush to reconstruct their war-flattened economy, Japanese businessmen relied on this cultural inheritance as they searched almost desperately for new ideas and technology.

Even today Japanese businessmen and government officials behave in such a way as to seek out the most advanced knowledge and techniques, blending and optimizing appropriately as they solve tough problems and discover how best to administer and manage their organizations.

The nation's sharp hunger for knowledge is not limited to large enterprises. Small business is also information-hungry. Unicharm, a company that has captured 60 percent of the sanitary napkin market after meteoric growth, wanted to diversify its business into paper diapers. Its first priority was to accumulate relevant foreign scientific and technological information. The company imported, for instance, a sample of the best starch developed by the U.S. Department of Agriculture to test its water absorbency and quality for possible application to the sensitive skin of Japanese babies.

The intellectual curiosity of the Japanese is of such intensity that it carries almost religious overtones when people approach the learning process. This is evident even in the activities of labor unions. The Isetan Labor Union organizes special New Year's seminars for all the union's executives, business representatives and shop stewards for three consecutive days every January. They invite top-notch economists, management consultants, negotiators, government officials, computer analysts, and consumer-interest representatives to sharpen their knowledge for the annual spring round of collective bargaining.

Because of the rigorous attitude that Japanese people bring to places of learning, I find it quite uncomfortable to begin my lectures with a joke, a customary practice in most countries outside Japan. This is because serious-minded Japanese audiences usually do not participate in educational activities with the expectation of being entertained.

Now Japan and other industrially advanced countries are caught up in a veritable information explosion. Peter Drucker's *Knowledge Society,* Daniel Bell's *Post-Industrial Society,* Alvin Tofler's *Third Wave,* and John Naisbitt's *Informative Society* are all household terms to most Japanese business people. Advanced electronics technology and various high technologies are about to substantially transform almost every aspect of Japanese life. And Japan's planned investment in this area of application is so great that people are being urged more than ever to unlearn previous knowledge and to acquire new knowledge in preparation for the approaching information revolution. In order to come up with better ways of tackling the challenge of the oncoming third generation of the postwar economic revolution, Japanese are being forced to re-evaluate their traditional approaches and to re-examine carefully some of the previous patterns of thought and innovation. The primary areas of concern which are topics of ardent discussion in Japan are the following:

1. Changing gears from information collectors to information providers

Kyodo News Agency, one of the two Japan-based news agencies, receives about 650,000 words of information daily from abroad and transmits them to client Japanese newspapers. The agency's daily dispatch from Japan, however, amounts to only 25,000 words. About 1,500 different books (primarily from American and European publishers) are translated into Japanese annually, but the reverse flow of Japanese books translated into other languages numbers a scant five dozen. Even a 75-year-old peasant woman in Japan can recite the names of ten Americans: Reagan, John Wayne, Marilyn Monroe, Washington, Lincoln, Edison, etc. It is unlikely, on the other hand, that the typical American mother could name any Japanese politicians or movie stars, with the possible exception of Emperor Hirohito and General Tojo. A recent survey conducted by Keio University's Institute of Newspaper Studies revealed that in the Massachusetts area some 25 percent of junior high school students think that Peking is the capital of Japan. Another study conducted in Europe revealed that the majority of senior high school students think that Japan is part of China and, furthermore, that it possesses atomic bombs (which it does not). This unfortunate discrepancy in the flow of information, which has generated severe perception gaps and contributed to Euro-Japan, U.S.-Japan trade frictions, must be rectified as soon as possible.

A well-balanced, two-way exchange of information is vital, and Japan must solve this problem to be able to make a real contribution to the global community.

We Japanese suffer not only from perception gaps between

ourselves and the world around us, but also from the new stereotypes brought on by economic success. Knowledgeable people abroad, for instance, believe that all Japanese employees enjoy lifetime employment, whereas in fact only about 25 percent of the Japanese labor force (primarily large-size enterprise employees) is protected by the permanent employment system. Many outsiders are also led to believe that Japanese wages are based solely on seniority, which is also untrue; more than 40 percent of wages and salaries are now determined by job classification, performance, and achievement.

2. The question of originality

Despite the success of the past and the expectation of continued success over the next twenty years, a growing concern among Japanese is whether Japan can base its future economic and technological growth on a repeat of its past performance as adaptor and emulator. Doubts about our ability to foster originality may haunt Japanese for some time to come — until, that is, we are able to devise creative means of generating genuine alternatives.

One of the favorite replies to this question is that Japanese group orientation may provide solutions through the joint sharing and probing of problems and enhancing the quality of "group thinking" as opposed to "group sinking."

3. Information — poverty amid the deluge

Returning to the earlier quantification of the volume of information — that average Japanese are continuously exposed every day of their lives to 2.3 quadrillion words of information — this flood of communications is largely "broadcast" in nature and is not guaranteed to reach the target population.

That is to say, only approximately one bit of information

out of 100 of this broadcast-type information reaches the intended audience. Information actually retained and used is only one-hundredth of that being transmitted. Therefore, from the viewpoint of value to senders, only about one out of ten thousand bits of information is actually utilized.

Thus despite the tremendous volume of knowledge and information circulated, actual use of information is extremely limited. Not only is there a serious waste of information, but people are also confronted by enormous quantities of conflicting information. There is a definite hunger for valid and usable knowledge amongst the information deluge. It is therefore becoming more and more important for citizens to be equipped with effective means for determining what is relevant and valid. They must sharpen the criteria employed in the process of selection to avoid being swallowed up in the flood which is constantly washing over them.

Prescription Plus Involvement

From the foregoing analysis, people abroad may be able to learn one vital lesson from the Japanese experience. One of the hidden secrets of the Japanese success may be the little-discussed, deep-rooted urge and motivation of the Japanese toward learning, their virtual obsession with upgrading and updating their knowledge. Whether or not this national trait is culture-bound or culture-free, in terms of application in other contexts, will require further exposition of Japanese behavior, values and culture. Some opponents may trace this propensity and emphasis on learning and education to the Confucian tradition, and point out a commonality to be found in the economic surges of Korea, Taiwan, Hong Kong, Singapore, and possibly in the not-too-distant future mainland China as well.

In terms of organizational development and "industrial

renaissance," even a good prescription provided by high-minded experts will not in itself guarantee effective performance. Unless it is coupled with a high degree of involvement and commitment on the part of the people concerned, no single prescription can function as effectively as might be hoped. It is true on the other hand, however, that even ideas and suggestions of lesser quality, when supported by a greater degree of involvement by those who are affected by and committed to their implementation, can generate a good amount of effective energy and produce striking results. Our Japanese answers, therefore, may prove more fruitful when transplanted across national borders if, in addition to a stronger sense of the importance of learning, they are pursued with a parallel sense of involvement.

The experiments in Singapore, which under the leadership of Minister Lee Kuan Yew, or in case of Malaysia under the "Look East" policy initiated by Prime Minister Mahathir Mohamad, are engaged in an attempt to learn from Japan, may offer an interesting case in point in the near future. The partial "Avisization" of American industry, in the words of Professor Ezra Vogel, and the recent upsurge of interest in absorbing new knowledge by laying hands on anything that might help U.S. industry regain its world competitiveness, combined with the U.S. economy's inherent resilience, will also provide a challenging test of the "transplantability" of the Japanese prescription embodied in a hunger for information plus an enthusiasm for learning.

The Aging and Affluent Nation

One major concern of most Japanese people today is the rapid aging of the population. The Japanese enjoy improved health and public sanitation and better nutrition than ever before, even though they eat only one-twentieth the beef and one-third the dairy products American consumers do. They now exercise more and have all the good things and all the bad things of America. They are faddish and try to import everything Americans have. One example is the craze triggered by the translation of Dr. Spock's book on child care. While some of this contributes to the raising of Japanese longevity above U.S. levels, the Japanese also have the tremendous task of accommodating a greater number of aging people within the time span of only 45 years, whereas it took from 75 to 170 years for most Western countries to get adjusted to these demographic changes. From the beginning of the 20th century until the end of World War II, the average life expectancy in Japan had been somewhere under 50 years. Now the average life expectancy is 73 years for males and 78 for females. The United Nations classifies countries with less than 4 percent of the population at 65 years or over as "young countries," and those having more than 7 percent in this age-bracket as "old countries." According to this definition, Japan became an "old country" in 1970. Although this quiet, invisible revolution did not arouse the Japanese public as keenly as the "Nixon shock" or the two "oil shocks," Japan is not yet ready — either socially or institutionally — to meet these drastic changes.

In order to illustrate this point, let me describe something I personally found quite shocking to observe. This sad example is the growing popularity of visits by old Japanese people, mostly women, to a temple in Nara in the central part of Japan, commonly known as Pokkuri Temple. *Pokkuri* means a sudden, peaceful death without any distress. It is sad to watch hundreds of elderly people earnestly praying to Buddha for a peaceful, sudden death without suffering from any protracted illness, and placing undergarments on the altar to symbolize their desire not to undergo pain and anguish. Observing this, I was reminded of a news item I read in *The New York Times* during my exchange-student years in New York City in the late 1950s. It concerned the diary of an old woman who had died and whose body had not been discovered for almost two weeks. She wrote, "No visitors today . . . Nobody called today . . . No friend visited today."

As a young student brought up in a close-knit family atmosphere, I could not at that time feel the urgency of the problem of loneliness and alienation among the elderly, but this is now a Japanese problem as well. There have been accelerated efforts to cope with the changes brought about by increased longevity. For instance, the Japanese government recently urged all employers to extend the compulsory retirement age of 55 to 60 or more, and the Advisory Council on Social Security recommended that the government itself raise the coverage of national pension schemes and expand recipients' benefits. Nevertheless, since postwar cultures have been primarily youth-oriented, it is still at the sacrifice of the middle-aged and elderly that the shift to form a new social order can be achieved. Therefore we can anticipate painful social readjustments for some time to come. For instance, 80 percent of the current Japanese unemployed are between the ages of 55 and 64, whereas in the United States the percentage is lower.

This issue dovetails the one of insensitive treatment of workers referred to as *madogiwa zoku*. *Madogiwa* means "by the window," and *zoku* means a group or type of people. They are the middle-aged and older workers who are, in a manner of speaking, on the ledge of the company organization regarded as "dead wood" — to be kicked out the window or laid off because the employers feel these workers can no longer be promoted in the company organization. On the more positive side, there are now so-called "silver and golden seminars," designed by the Mitsubishi Electric Enterprise Union to help assess problems of middle-aged and elderly union members and to help them redefine their life goals and career goals as well as cope with middle-age stress.

The Japanese have found themselves in a very awkward position all of a sudden, with everyone in the world telling them repeatedly that Japan is an economic superpower. Although Japan is an affluent country, enjoying one of the highest GNPs per capita in the free world, Japanese are perplexed because they do not feel all that affluent. This perception gap is very real, at least to the Japanese. Japanese homes are equipped with all kinds of electrical appliances. Last year almost 4.2 million

Japanese traveled abroad and bought all sorts of luxury items and ate at some three hundred Japanese restaurants now existing in New York. There is no escaping these facts, but the Japanese cannot believe they are actually affluent.

A confidential report of the European Economic Community is said to have described Japan as "a nation of workaholics who live in what Westerners could regard as little more than rabbit hutches." Undoubtedly, many Japanese were furious at the racist undertone of this report, but I could sympathize with the Europeans' frustration which apparently stems from Japan's substantial trade with them. The harsh evaluation concerning rabbit hutches is quite valid: the so-called affluence of the Japanese is only skin-deep. It is a superficial, fragile prosperity. Japan still has comparatively poorly paved roads, the sewage system is still underdeveloped, and there is relatively little space for living and for public parks. Therefore, as far as the amenities of life and decent living conditions are concerned, Japan remains far behind "civilized" Western countries. It is in this area that Japan must work very hard to build a pleasant living environment and guarantee a stable livelihood through the establishment of a decent, meaningful social security system.

Organization Development in Japan

In Collaboration with W. Warner Burke

Japanese are the most skillful imitators in the world. It has been said that with some products their copy is superior to the original. Transporting and copying "products" that pertain to human behavior and culture is quite another matter. Importing an idea or approach to change in behavior requires modification and adaptation especially when two cultures are as different as the United States and Japan. And so it has been with organization development (OD). As conceived in the United States OD was first introduced in Japan around 1965 and, just as in the United States, evolved from sensitivity training. Today, however, OD in Japan is in the process of forming its own shape and establishing unique characteristics. For example, the generally accepted definition of OD in Japan is similar to the more popular ones in the United States but differs in at least two significant ways. OD in Japan is "a process of planned change which attempts to integrate individual needs for growth with organizational objectives by using knowledge and techniques from the behavioral sciences." This definition is quite compatible with those used in the United States but differs from perhaps the most popular definition in that no mention is made of either "system-wide change effort" or "managed from the top." Explaining this difference as well as others and providing an overview of the distinctive characteristics of OD in Japan constitute the primary purposes of this article.

Why OD in Japan

During the past five years OD has steadily gained popularity and importance, particularly in business/industry among personnel specialists and training directors. Gradually OD is being accepted by top management and middle managers, especially those in companies which are international. Japan's international business and the spread of multinational companies has increased significantly in recent years, despite the recessions. Direct investments abroad by Japanese companies amounted to 6 billion dollars in 1972. Two years later this figure had doubled and by 1985 the total overseas investment figure is expected to be 60 billion dollars.

Historically, however, Japanese management has been relatively and therefore not particularly knowledgeable regarding the complexities of dealing with other cultures. And, in recent times, they have experienced difficulties in their relations with others even to the point of being labeled "ugly" — as some American were in years past. Japanese managers are looking for more assistance in the human domain. Organization development, particularly with its view of an organization as having a distinct culture like a nation or society, is seen as one response to these more complicated human problems.

Other more specific reasons for this growing acceptance can

be explained in terms of OD practitioners, providing a response or perhaps a solution to some problems with other approaches to organizational improvement, and certain inherent subsystems in the Japanese organization.

Something Wrong with MBO

OD has been seen as a breakthrough in revitalizing programs of management by objectives (MBO). Incidentally, the second author has encountered this same reason for initiating OD in an agency of the Canadian government.

Inspired by Peter Drucker's *The Practice of Management*, which sold close to 3 million copies in translation, Japanese personnel and training specialists pursued MBO as a way of improving the management of their organizations. In Japan today, however, MBO is near bankruptcy. There are at least three reasons for this decline:

• Followers of MBO had a tendency to promote merely a ready-made system of forms to fill out rather than a process of change in management. (It is ironic that the Japanese abbreviation for MBO is *"mokkan"* which sounds like "mocking," or mokuhyo-niyoru-kanri which connotes an empty wooden tube.)

• Managers were encouraged simply to list plausible goals and objectives with little or no attention being paid to how they would be implemented.

• Proponents of MBO did not pay adequate attention to the culture or climate of the organization when attempting to bring about this change in management practice.

Unfortunately, MBO in Japan has deteriorated to "Management by Obstruction," "Management by Obsession," or "Management by Obtrusion." Thus, OD comes as a viable option for revitalizing attempts to reach the same kinds of change objectives as those of MBO.

Something Wrong with Sensitivity Training

OD has been seen as an effective series of follow-up activities for management development, in general, and laboratory or sensitivity training, in particular. Sensitivity training in Japan has been limited to individual development and not designed to include dimensions of group, intergroup, and organizational behavior. Management development and other forms of training have not affected organizations in any measurable way. This lack of impact is no doubt due to training specialists' staying with the questionable assumption that an organization can be changed and improved by training organizational members to perform differently. These trainers have begun to realize that an individual strategy of change, i.e., if you improve the person the organization thereby will be improved, has limitations. Without organizational support for the objectives of a training effort, the effects of the training will dissipate or have no organizational impact at all. Training directors in U.S. organizations need to understand this as well.

Something Wrong with Work Improvement Groups

OD has been seen as a way to strengthen the variety of small group activities in Japanese organizations. In almost any Japanese work environment in the large and medium-size business/industrial organizations, one will find a diversity of small work improvement groups. They exist under a variety of names such as quality control circle, industrial engineering study group, zero defect group, or suggestion system study group, and they are usually formed on a voluntary basis. These groups are endorsed by management but are often subtly manipulated to meet desired ends of the organizations, at least as interpreted by key managers. Nevertheless, these work improvement groups have played an important role in encouraging rank and file participation to improve productivity and quality, reduce cost and enhance morale.

From time to time these groups become stale and need new problems and ideas to consider or, at least, new approaches. OD activities such as team building have become useful as renewal efforts for work improvement groups.

Something Wrong with the System

OD has been seen as a means of revitalizing sluggish and outmoded organizational systems and structures. Recently there has been a sense of urgency at all levels of management, especially those from the larger and older businesses, to convert traditional Japanese management approaches into more dynamic ones in order to be more responsive to a rapidly changing environment. In light of an increasing number of dissatisfied consumers, more attention being paid to ecology and to a higher quality of work life, less "workaholic" attitudes among younger employees, more mobility of workers, and increased contacts with other cultures as a result of an accelerated internationalization of Japanese industries, managers have felt a keen need to change their organizations:

• from largely bureaucratic systems to consumer- and employee-oriented operations,

• from role and status orientations to a task orientation, and

• from rigidity in organizational structure to more flexibility.

With an impetus toward organizational change, in any case, OD is beginning to be adopted as a more systematic way of improvement since the emphasis is on planned change.

To set the stage and provide a background for comparing OD in Japan with that of the United States, we shall now turn to a discussion of some of the unique characteristics of Japanese management.

Characteristics of Organizational Behavior in Japan

In order to appreciate and understand Japanese OD efforts, we shall provide a comparison of Japanese and U.S. values and behavior within the context of their respective organizations. Presented in Exhibit 1 is a summary of some of the more salient characteristics for comparison. We shall now consider in some detail only the more important dimensions.

Groupism

The Japanese are a group-oriented society. Take, for example, a group of tourists at a restaurant ordering breakfast. From the waiter's or waitress' point of view taking orders from a group of Americans is no small matter. They will be highly particular in tastes and desires from one individual to another. Some will want coffee immediately, others later. Some will prefer orange juice, a few a large glass, the rest a small one while others will want grapefruit juice.

Japanese in the same situation will behave quite the opposite. The waiter or waitress will have to consult the leader of the tourist group to receive a rather nonspecific order which miraculously applies to everyone. The leader will likely say, "Oh, whatever you think would be appropriate for this party," or "whatever the chef recommends," or whatever the leader decides for himself will somehow fit the entire group. Japanese like to call this simplicity and conformity of handling a group of tourists a "set-menu efficiency."

This mentality, which Professor Hiroshi Hazama has labeled "groupism," is probably the most distinguishing characteristic of the Japanese personality structure. It is never

A Comparison of Organizational Behavior Between Japanese and U.S. Personnel

Characteristic	United States	Japan
Personal emphasis	Individualism (I, me) "Lone wolf" personality	Groupism (part of we) "Band wagon" personality
Interpersonal relationships	Independence encouraged	Mutual dependence encouraged
Worker participation	Less Competition Elitism	More Collaboration Egalitarianism
Competence	Ability (talent) Specialist preferred	Total personality Generalist preferred
Decision making	Top-down Quick Individualistic	Bottom- or middle-up Slow Consensual
Conflict	To be confronted and surfaced Emphasis on conflict management	To be avoided or "melted" through *nemawashi* Emphasis on agreement management
Communication	Verbal and written	Nonverbal and implied
Sense of belonging/Loyalty	Low	High
Nature of change	Abrupt Complete Surgical	Evolutionary Renew or repair Massage not surgery
Basis of employment and promotion	On merit	Life-long employment Seniroty

overlooked nor underestimated by the Japanese. The clearest example of how this mentality is manifested in organizational life is in decision-making. As a rule, decisions are made by consensus. In U.S. organizations this is the exception. Japanese, therefore, typically take more time in decision making, but less time in implementation. For Americans the reverse appears to be the case.

Ambiguity and Flexibility

The person who has a very low tolerance for ambiguity would have a tough time in the Japanese organization. According to a study conducted by a Japanese student at International Christian University in Tokyo, there are currently some 19 different ways for the Japanese to say "no." As a Japanese manager transplanted by Mitsubishi Corporation to one of its subsidiary plants in Texas expressed it, "I've had to learn to say 'no' instead of 'that's very difficult.' "

The U.S. manner of being more straightforward and "telling it like it is" sometimes causes conflict between boss and subordinate or among peers. Japanese see this kind of behavior as creating conditions for "losing face," an outcome they work to avoid. Keeping conditions ambiguous allows for face saving.

Japanese have many rules, regulations, and policies but as long as the interpretation of these norms and their implementation can be left vague, organizational members can relate to one another with less strain and frustration. For the American this ambiguity often has the opposite effect.

Interwoven closely with ambiguity is flexibility, another marked feature of the Japanese character. This behavioral characteristic is reflected in the continued popularity of the traditional kimono. This robe of typically cotton fabric requires no other garments for appropriate wear, is highly economical, and is convenient for either sex. Since it has wide front panels which overlap, the kimono is comfortable for a midriff of any circumference.

Examples within the Japanese organization include (a) the Sohmu ("general affairs") department, a "permanent task force" which exists in most organizations for the purpose of taking care of random assignments, i.e., those tasks which need attention but do not fit within any existing organizational function, and (b) job rotation for managers. With respect to the latter, it is Japanese custom for a manager to work toward becoming a generalist rather than maintain a particular specialty. To facilitate this development, managers rotate from one area of specialization to another. Moreover, if a person wants to progress to the ranks of top management, he must work for several years in, say, personnel, even though his original training may have been engineering. It is an exception for the chief executive of a U.S. company to have previously been the head of corporate personnel and prior to that a plant manager.

Nature of Change

Change in U.S. organizations is typically "out with the old, in with the new," that is, when change does occur it is often abrupt and little if any of the previous ways, or perhaps people, remain. The older situation is negated or abolished in order to build a new one. In Japan change occurs by overlapping the old system with the new, i.e., evolution not revolution. The old is never completely eliminated. The process of assimilation is most important. For example, when a manager is not performing his job competently he is rarely, if ever, fired; rather, he is transferred to some other function and thereby is retained in the organization.

In U.S. organizations one system for, say, management information which has become ineffective will typically be replaced entirely with a new one. The new system may be a better approach but not work any more effectively at least initially, due to the amount of re-learning required. In Japanese organizations the previous system will usually be augmented rather than eliminated. Learning an entirely new system is not a problem. The problem is that these modified systems may become compounded and therefore more complex to implement.

Jitsuryoku

Social classes do exist in Japanese society but they are ambiguous. What is more important for upward mobility than social class, however, is the combination of power and interpersonal sensitivity. The Japanese word, *jitsuryoku*, conveys this combination in human behavior. One who is competent, say, in business, and at the same time has modesty, humility, and interpersonal sensitivity has *jitsuryoku*. With *jitsuryoku*, then, one has a good chance of moving up in the Japanese organization. When visiting a Japanese factory it is often difficult to determine who the boss is. Everyone wears the same uniform and eats in the same cafeteria. For example the Japanese chief executive of YKK's fastener plant in Macon, Georgia wears the company's uniform jacket, and often works an hour or so each day as a machine operator.

Top management personnel in Japanese organizations do have their status and privileges, but they do not appear to maintain them quite as imperiously as U.S. top management.

OD Japanese Style

Applied behavioral science is not new to Japan even though OD as such has a history of no more than five years. Previous translations of many books in the behavioral sciences have helped to pave the way for the more recent acceptance of OD. Most of the major works of people like Lewin, McGregor, Mayo and Roethlisburger have been translated. In addition, Argyris, Herzberg, Likert, Maslow, McClelland and Blanchard are familiar names to Japanese personnel specialists, training directors, and OD practitioners. Blake and Mouton formed a joint venture company in Japan to promote the Managerial Grid, and BNA's films on management and applied behavioral science have been dubbed in Japanese.

Originally, the NTL Institute of Applied Behavioral Science jointly sponsored with Business Consultants, Inc., the Japan Institute of Christian Education, and the Institute of Business Management a number of laboratory training programs and OD seminars and workshops. These programs have helped to

- provide the theoretical basis for OD practice,
- clarify the differences between sensitivity training and OD, and
- encourage interaction and exchange of OD specialists in both countries.

As a way of providing more specific information about OD in Japan, a comparative approach will again be used. Exhibit 2 summarizes the explanation that follows.

History

OD has existed in the United States for almost 15 years whereas in Japan the practice is less than five years old. In the United States, it is generally agreed that OD stemmed from two roots, the survey feedback approach to organization diagnosis and change developed at the University of Michigan's Institute for Social Research, and the laboratory training method developed by the NTL Institute. In Japan, OD has emerged essentially from sensitivity training, in particular, and

A Comparison of Organization Development in Japan and the U.S.A.

Comparative Dimension	United States	Japan
History	Approximately 15 years Roots: Sensitivity training and survey/feedback	Five years or less Roots: Sensitivity training
Approach	Consultant centered	Training centered
Consultants	Outside consultants utilized	Inside consultants preferred
Organizations involved in Organization Development	Variety including non-business/industrial	Middle and lower management
Primary values advocated	Openness and authenticity	Harmony and mutual dependence
Diagnostic bias	Managerial style	*Tatemae* (should be) vs. *Hon-ne* (what is)
Diagnostic behavior	Shallow Quick to take action, intervene	Perfectionistic Methodical "Analysis paralysis"
Interventions	Eclectic Tailor made Experimental	Tried and true techniques Limited number

experience-based training, in general.

This emergence of OD in Japan from training is understandable in that the country's business/industrial organizations have been on a very fast track over the past 30 years with many people, particularly managers, who required training in a hurry. This requirement for a large number of lightly trained managers has, of course, spawned legions of training specialists. Many of the "people specialists" in Japanese organizations are therefore trainers or closely associated with training.

Approach

Based on the historical development of OD in Japan it is not surprising that the primary approach of most practitioners is from a training base. What Japanese practitioners attempt to do initially is develop a training program for their client. This is well received since training in Japanese organizations has considerable legitimacy. This is probably not as true in the United States. The Japanese trainer/consultant then attempts to add another element of OD like team building as a follow-up to his training program.

The approach in the United States is more consultatively centered with a problem-solving emphasis. An alternative solution to the problem as initially diagnosed may be a training program but, more than likely, the step that is taken is in some other area of OD interventions, e.g., conflict management or job enrichment.

Consultants

Although the trend seems to be changing, especially during times of economic difficulties, there has been in the past a bias in the United States to rely rather heavily on outside consultants for OD work. In Japan the number of external OD consultants at present are few indeed; perhaps no more than a dozen. Therefore, again the emphasis has been on training; in this case the training of certain organizational members, typically from personnel and/or training, to be OD specialists.

A partial explanation of this difference between the United States and Japan is how each country's academic people operate. It is no doubt safe to conclude that a large number of OD consultants come from universities. In the United States college professors, especially those who are faculty members of schools of business and management, supplement their university salaries by consulting. Thus, there are many outside OD consultants, or at least potential ones, on the market. In Japan, college professors are more concerned with their theories. There is considerably less emphasis on applying one's scholarship. The market for external OD consultants is therefore limited from the supply side.

Organizations

OD in the United States has been extended to a variety of organizations. While business/industrial organizations still remain in the majority, government and nonprofit service organizations, particularly in the health services, have become considerably more active in OD within the last three or four years. In Japan OD is limited almost exclusively to business/industry. In the early days of OD in the United States this was also the case. It may be that in the near future OD in Japan as previously in the United States will begin to expand to nonbusiness organizations.

Management Levels

Although all OD efforts in the United States do not start from top management most OD practitioners attempt to include the top managers, particularly the chief executive officer, as soon as possible. This approach is based on the fact that for U.S. organizations the management process is usually top-down. In Japan, management is not typically top-down. Operational management is carried out by middle and lower levels. Thus, OD in Japan concentrates primarily on middle managers on down, including the rank and file.

Primary Values

OD practiced in the United States emphasizes openness, candor and "owning up" in the communication processes of organizations. A related and recent trend stressed by U.S. practitioners of OD is one of managers' paying more attention to who they are rather than what they might become. In other words, the emphasis is on understanding more about one's unique pattern of personality characteristics, strengths and competencies and capitalizing more on these aspects of behavior rather than attempting to adopt a specific managerial style which may not fit one's particular personality and unique set of talents.

In Japan the emphasis is definitely not on openness and candor. In the interest of not hurting one another's feelings, Japanese work hard at maintaining harmony and interacting with one another as cooperatively as possible. Moreover, Japanese interact in a mutually dependent manner. For example, it is expected that people regardless of organizational rank or responsibility will voluntarily pitch in and help one another with their jobs. A waiter or waitress in a Japanese restaurant does not have a specific table that he or she serves exclusively. Everyone serves all tables. It is a norm among the Japanese that they do not ask for help; it is expected that help will come when needed because everyone is socialized to be sensitive to others' needs. Teamwork, then, is paramount. This accounts for the fact that team-building is the most popular OD intervention.

Diagnostic Bias

OD practitioners in the United States tend to find something wrong with the managerial style of individual managers, or with the managerial characteristic of the organization as a whole. There are exceptions to this bias, and it may be that there is now a swing away from this emphasis. Nevertheless, the bias has dominated OD in the United States for most of its 15-year history.

In Japan there is typically a gap between what is formally and publicly espoused *(Tatemae)* and what people actually believe and desire *(Hon-ne)*. The OD practitioner therefore typically begins his diagnostic effort by trying to decipher what official policy is from what organizational members in reality portray in their behavior. This is a difficult process, for Japanese are masters at masking their feelings, opinions and motives. Thus, it is common practice for the OD practitioner to spend time in a Ginza bar with his client as a primary way of discovering what he (the client) really believes and feels. It should be added that this practice is not exactly foreign behavior to the U.S. OD practitioner.

Diagnostic Behavior

OD practitioners in Japan are drawn largely from staff functions, primarily personnel and training. Japanese staff work is meticulous, methodical and detailed. The staff person's work must leave room for few questions, at least none that cannot be answered. In OD, therefore, he tends to approach organizational diagnosis in much the same way. The Japanese person who aspires to OD specialization is probably frustrated with the discovery that team or organizational diagnosis can never be final or complete. As a consultant, he is faced with a living system that is dynamic, ever moving, and perhaps "slippery" in the sense that when he feels he finally has his hands on the system, it begins to slip away from him. Under these conditions the Japanese OD consultant becomes immobilized, unable or unwilling to take action because his diagnosis is partial, not complete. Meanwhile, his client is wondering if help will ever come.

Since the client organization is not precisely the same at the time of diagnostic report (feedback) as it was at the time of data collection, a diagnosis that is too complete may not be accurate. Moreover, a diagnostic report that is too complete may come across to the client as "mechanical," with no consideration of the fact that the client has feelings.

The U.S. practitioner on the other hand is frequently not thorough enough in a diagnosis before he takes action. The culture of U.S. business/industrial organization is characterized by rapid action planning, decisiveness, and movement. Thus, the U.S. OD specialist tends to take action, to make an intervention, which is based on diagnostic information that is often too shallow.

This cross-cultural contrast is oversimplified and stereotypical, but the behavioral tendencies are fairly obvious nevertheless. The field of OD would undoubtedly gain if the two cultures could borrow from one another.

Interventions

OD interventions in the United States are varied, some predesigned, and others evolve as a result of certain diagnoses. In Japan OD interventions are limited in number and practitioners prefer to stick with techniques that are well known, relatively

37

easy to understand and implement, and compatible with Japanese values. Team-building is used most widely due to its support of teamwork values, and long history of practice in the United States. Another technique which is growing in popularity is "organization mirror," a process whereby one organizational unit, say, computer services, receives feedback from other units which it serves as to the effectiveness of or problems with the services provided.

Japanese practitioners rely rather heavily on questionnaires, especially scale-type surveys where data can be quantified. They use visual aids whenever possible, especially wall charts with graphs and percentiles.

Conclusions

Organization development is not a process of change for the sake of change, and Japanese managers and OD practitioners would do well to consider with care what aspects of their culture manifested in organization behavior should not only remain but be reinforced. For example, emphasizing consensual decision-making and the direct involvement of managers with the rank and file are assets. OD U.S. style can contribute little to these strengths. Perhaps the two primary ways that OD as conceived and developed in the United States can contribute to Japanese organizations are

- considering organization diagnosis from a cultural frame of reference, i.e., viewing an organization as having a culture just as a society or nation has, and
- providing a greater variety of OD interventions.

With time it is likely that OD in Japan will be characterized more by how it differs from the original imported version than by how it is similar. Moreover, OD in Japan is rapidly being adapted to the Japanese culture. This adaptation seems to be predominantly a function of value differences, as would be expected. The fact that candor in interpersonal affairs is not exactly the way of life in Japan, and is not likely to be in the future, means that the practice of OD will be taking considerably different forms.

The Future of OD in Japan

Japan's expansion into the world marketplace is, of course, modern history. And her expansion has been truly remarkable. As noted by Drucker, Japan is today among the handful of nations (eight to be exact) where 95 percent of the world's multinational corporations are domiciled. The other seven countries are the United States and six Western European nations. For world business, then, Japan culturally speaking, is unique. Japan has at least 450 joint venture companies in Brazil alone; 5,000 Japanese live in Dusseldorf, West Germany, 4,500 in London, and more than 22,000 in New York City. Operating effectively in cultures quite different from her own is key to Japan's economic future. The fact that many practitioners and writers in the field view organization development as a process of cultural change may facilitate the work required.

More specifically, a major cross-cultural dynamic that Japanese OD practitioners will have to understand and deal with is the fact that most of the rest of the world is not as clannish, clubby, and group-oriented as they are. From the standpoint of OD practice inside Japanese organizations this cultural norm is, in many respects, an advantage. A strong bias of OD over the years has been that of participation and involvement, and this bias and approach has easily been adopted and improved upon by the Japanese. But value and managerial preferences in other parts of the world are not as participative. With the possible exception of England and the Scandinavian countries with their trend toward industrial democracy, most of Europe's value orientations in organizations are in the direction of power and authority. And in the United States top priority is accomplishment of the task; people considerations are subordinated to the task.

Be these differences as they may, Japan is highly dependent on other countries for its resources; therefore, multinational corporations (MNCs) from Japan will have growing impact in the world both in so-called advanced countries and in those labeled as developing. Moreover, due to sharp increases in wages Japan is moving more toward hiring local people in other countries, especially where labor is cheap.

Domestically, Japanese OD must tackle the changing work ethics and values of the younger and better-educated workers. These young people are more inclined than their elders toward greater mobility, higher quality of working life, more leisure, and greater opportunities for self-actualization in a shorter span of time.

In short, Japan is now on the threshold of yet greater changes in society. Japan's people have demonstrated to themselves and to the world that they are world leaders in the industrial and economic marketplace. Now, to maintain that leadership, Japan's managers must learn how to live and work in different cultures. This learning is imperative due to Japan's

- GNP now increasingly dependent on international business and thereby her MNCs, and
  - severe import demands, e.g., oil.

Perhaps more than any other country in the world in terms of economic survival Japan must be an integral part of and leader within the world marketplace. It is therefore in Japan's interest to understand social systems more from a cultural if not social psychological frame of reference. Learning more about organization development in particular will facilitate this understanding.

Productivity and Japanese Management Style

Interviewer: Meyer Michael Cahn, Ed.D.

Cahn, Douglas Associates, Inc.,
San Francisco, California

Cahn: The first questions I'd like to ask you, Maurie,* concern a Japanese perspective of American management. You occupy an unusual position in that you not only know Japanese management, and consultatively help Japanese management, but you also have a pretty good idea of our own American management style and our own literature. You translate American books on management, you frequently attend American management conferences, and you consult in the U.S. So the first question, then, is this: How do American management and American organizational administration look from the perspective of students of management in Japan? How do we look from here in Tokyo?

Kobayashi: Well, I might take the risk of over-simplification or over-generalization; but we see American management, American organizational practices—here on this side of the

―――――――――
* Professor Kobayashi enjoys being called "Maurie."

Pacific (I commute across the Pacific very often)—putting too much emphasis on the individualistic approaches, whereas we place too much emphasis on group dependence, or interdependence. Shall I elaborate a little further now?

C: Fine.

INDIVIDUALISM VS. GROUPISM:

K: My favorite way to explain the different approaches in management and organization behavior—your individualistic approaches or our group directiveness—can be explained this way. Suppose 50 businessmen are traveling on tour together. To order their breakfast in a typical restaurant in a hotel—where self-service or cafeteria service is not available—you, the American people try to order specifically according to your own taste. The waiter, accordingly, will have to ask each individual for their own preference, for what type of food they want to have. They usually ask you if you want your coffee now or later. And they ask if you want to order juice—orange, tomato or grapefruit. And they have to specify whether you want a large or a small one. And they ask how do you want your eggs? Fried? Boiled? And then, do you want some meat with it? So you specify what kind of meat you want. And if you want bacon you have to specify if you want the bacon to be crisp or not. This takes, say, one minute to take each order. Multiplied by 50, shall we say, it will take 50 minutes for taking orders.

In Japan, in the same situation, you don't have to worry about taking 50 minutes for taking the breakfast order of a group of 50. The waiter just goes to the leader, or escort or courier and asks him what the group wants. His answer is usually "Whatever you say fits." So group effectiveness must come first, at the risk of the individual appetite.

So, then, scrambled eggs come and I find I don't like the

scrambled eggs—I personally like fried eggs—but everybody is eating scrambled eggs. So our group preference or orientation seems to be our strength as well as our weakness. Sometimes it tends to become counter-productive. So this seems to be one of the salient differences.

I might give you one more example to illustrate the point. You have been in Japan for some time, now, and have observed that the Japanese people like a box lunch. Japanese box lunches are somewhat different from your box lunches. They are compartmentalized, they have about 10 or 11 compartments in their box lunches. And you can have some pieces of chicken, some pieces of vegetable, pieces of egg, two pieces of fish, of eel, octopus, whatever you say. So there is the possibility of one of the people in the organization having at least a part of his desire in this compartmentalized, set-menu box lunch. He may not be satisfied with the fish, but he may find some gratification in having at least one of his favorite foods—say, the octopus. So partial satisfaction is always guaranteed in box lunch types of approaches, whereas you prefer the one, individualistic approach—steak or roast beef. It is a very indirect way of describing organization behavior, but is the way I perceive it.

C: So in your last example about the box lunch, there is a concern for individual satisfaction. But integrating the individual with the group is even more paramount.

K: Yes, indeed.

C: In asking for your comment about American management, then, the first difference would be individualism and, one might say, groupism. Perhaps another way I might ask this question is to to ask what you see as our greatest strength, or strengths. You have mentioned individualism. In what way do you see this individualism as a strength?

K: Instead of answering your question directly in the American situation, I might answer how the group orientation sometimes acts counter-productively, in terms of the whole organization or a bigger dynamism. Japanese younger people after the end of World War II have been trained to be more expressive and articulate not necessarily to conform to the group norms. They have also been encouraged to be more aggressive.

SOME EXTERNAL INFLUENCES:
C: Who has encouraged them to be more aggressive?
K: After the end of the war there was a tremendous impact of the American approaches in the educational system, from the primary school through the junior high and senior high. And also the change of the educational system tended to democratize. Also, there has been tremendous contact with the outer world.

More than 4 million Japanese people traveled abroad last year. There are about 12,000 Japan-based companies all over the world, companies of Japanese origin. There are 530 Japanese-owned companies in the state of California. For instance, in Los Angles there are about 5,000 Japanese businessmen working as expatriate resident directors or managers. In Brazil, there are 630 Japanese companies operating, including some nominal small companies. Now there are Japanese companies employing more than 1.2 million people throughout the world in local employment. So this international contact has had a tremendous impact. Also, we have the highly advanced knowledge/information industry. We have learned, and particularly younger people have learned, to be more expressive, to be more aggressive. They are recruited by the large business and governmental organizations... Mitsui, Mitsubishi... and then they get quite frustrated because they have to go up the ladder of success. If you want to reach the first and second level you have to wait five or ten years. To be promoted to manager you have to wait at least ten years. So if the younger people have a yearning or desire to fill a higher position, to become more influential, to achieve something else, they get quite frustrated. Whereas in the U.S. the aggressive younger people who are intelligent enough, and experienced, could find the better places to work on their own program of ambitions. One of the largest American banks operating in Japan, where I have been working, has this problem. The younger people have a dilemma. On the one hand they have to encourage, according to the principles of American management, the up-coming of the younger people, whereas also they have to pay enough attention to the people who have not necessarily reached the level of incompetence just as Peter (the Peter Principle) says. The combination is quite a delicate problem.

U.S. STRENGTHS (MANAGEMENT):
C: So one strength you see in American management is the ability to move bright, talented people along, and not have to hold them back, not have them frustrated. . .
K: . . . So that they will be able to explore their potential at much earlier stages.
C: . . . and to bring their talents into the organization. What are some other strengths of American management?
K: One of the strengths of American management is the fact that you are allowed to hire or fire at the discretion of the top executive management when the business is going down. In Japan, because of the long history of the family approach, the loving care approach, the paternalistic concern, because of the seniority-based wage system, because of the permanent employment commitment—it is quite difficult to do this when the business is going down and the organization is having some difficulties. We cannot fire the redundant or unnecessary personnel

easily. It is almost impossible. The lay-off is almost the very last resort in the typical large and established Japanese organization. So when business suffers, like the surgeons, you (in the U.S.) can quickly cut off, you can very quickly undertake a very drastic operation, and by that means, you will be able to be viable and survive in a very harsh environment. In Japan it takes more time, because they are not well trained to get rid of people; instead of giving a kind of shot or surgical operation in the Japanese company, they try to provide herb medicines or try to stimulate the whole function of the body. So in the short term basis, when the environment is very detrimental, or difficult for the organization, you can easily save and salvage certain organizations or entities in the U.S. But sometimes we find it almost impossible.

VOLUME PRODUCTION AND SURVIVAL:

C: That leads me to a question I was going to ask later, but I think it may fit in now. Does this explain perhaps why there is a Japanese proclivity for volume production, and also why one senses aggressive expansion effort on the part of Japanese organizations? In other words, inasmuch as they may be faced with a decline of revenue—or in the lower ends of cycles—one way out of that dilemma, and the personnel point which you make, would be to be rather aggressive in expansion—in volume, to gain new markets and to extend other markets? Does this explain such actions?

K: Right. Those are reasons. I think that is valid. And also, we have a kind of obsession for survival because of our limited material resources.

Almost 100 percent of the bauxite and aluminum comes from abroad. Our energy . . . 90 percent comes from the outside . . . and oil. We have no cotton. All the cotton comes from India or Egypt. We have almost no wheat so we have to import mostly from the U.S. About 68 percent of the lumber is from Canada, the Philippines or Indonesia. So far as natural resources are concerned, for our chauvinistic survival, we are very much concerned. There is constant fear and anxiety for survival because of the shortage of natural resources. So we are always driven to go abroad, sometimes just to flood the market, shall we say—an aggressive volume approach. Together with your explanation, it seems to me we have to point out that there seems to be felt a deep-rooted anxiety for survival because of the limitations of the natural resources.

C: That is certainly understandable. That expression "obsession for survival" is an interesting one, and I think it explains much that we see. Certainly in America we are particularly endowed with rich resources.

K: For instance, in making an analysis of the GNP structure of the United States, about 63 percent of your gross national product is your domestic, individual consumption. In Japan, the domestic consumption constitutes about 50 percent. So you have a vast market.

C: An internal market.

K: And 25 times more area than we have. So you don't have to worry about going aggressively abroad. You have abundant potential in your own domestic market. You just cultivate the back of your gardens and you find oil.

U.S. COMPLACENCY AND RESILIENCY:
C: Do you think, then, that that leads to some of the complacency that I personally find in America at this time? This is 1980, the beginning of a new administration, inflation is high, there is an economic downturn. And there is a sense of negativity running throughout the country, an economic sense of

negativity. Do you believe that some of this very richness that you described, and that we have, leads to some of this complacency?

K: I think my answer is yes and no. Some Japanese commentators, economists or businessmen, have been saying that Americans have been complacent. Particularly after the devastating nightmares of Vietnam, you seem to have lost the confidence as an international leader—and the decline of productivity. There are many dilemmas and problems posed internationally. You're lost in the American dream. Also the macho complex is coming up again . . . especially waiting for the new strong leaders. To those people who have been saying that there is nothing to learn from America anymore . . . who say that the American Age is gone, I usually just say, "Now listen. You have to be very careful. I don't think you can say that."

The seeming complacency of the U.S. is not a long term problem. In the short term, yes. In the long term the American society has very strong potential and dynamic vigor.

For instance, you have problems which we don't have. As I see the American organization, if something comes up, usually there are strong countervailing powers that are operating. If something comes up and you have adverse relations—you know, if some power and anti-power comes up—this whole process of the swinging of the pendulum from one way to the other, you have a resilience. This is American.

When Mr. Reagan was elected there was a movement that was considered by President Carter and Professor Etzioni and these Democratic people, as the re-industrialization of the U.S. That is another healthy sign of the counter-active movement, to try to heal the American difficulties. To those people who say the American Age is gone, I just say that this is quite wrong. We must be careful not to make oversimplified statements.

On the other hand, in Japan we also have our vulnerable areas. We are very fragile in a way. Some of the people who highly praise Japanese productivity, Japanese quality, the Japanese quality circle movement, autonomous groups—this is getting kind of faddish—but we also have our problems and they have not been successfully solved yet.

CONFRONTING PROBLEMS:

C: It seems to me that you may be saying that there is a virtue in the American ability to confront problems more directly. In my readings, I have particularly noticed that confrontation (and you point this out in one of your own articles) is not a characteristic of Japanese management style.

K: Not on the surface. (Laughter)

C: That is a very important point you are making. It is there, all right. In nonverbal ways?

K: But suppressed. We have our conflict and confrontation, but it is suppressed. We are not supposed to surface a confrontation. We've got to pretend that everything is all right.

Confrontation is the name of the game in American organizations and through this confrontation—even though it may not be good for your heart—all the problems are clear. Power confrontation is sometimes very healthy, because you can clearly identify the issues and problems.

Even though we have our conflicts and problems, we have been trained not to call a spade a spade; so we try to pretend that we do not have any problems, which is quite dangerous—unless a wise leader can identify the problem and change the organization through the very painstaking *nemawashi* way. *Nemawashi* is the name of a root. It means going around.

If you want to do something in the Japanese business conference, you have to do some groundwork. Unless you have some informal discussion beforehand, you will never be able to succeed at a meeting. I may be exaggerating, but usually a meeting in the U.S. is someplace where you have to "win." Meeting here is some kind of post approval, something already decided behind the scenes. It is staged before.

Jerry Harvey (Georgetown University management professor) came here and said what you need is conflict in management, but what we need is "agreement management." We have too much pseudo agreement. We have to crush and destroy this complacence, so much buddy-buddy type of not genuine agreement, whereas you need more coordinated approaches. I think that he has a very good point.

CRITICIZING JAPANESE MANAGEMENT:
C: We manage our conflict. You manage your agreement. I want to make a comment about this part of our discussion, Maurie. Now you have been a little bit critical of Japanese management style. Is there any personal risk, or professional risk in being a critic of Japanese management?
K: No. Not at all. They enjoy it.
C: Your colleagues enjoy it?
K: Yes. We have a saying in Japan: Generally, OK. On principle OK. Specifically, *no!*
C: (Laughter) That ends up being *nothing*.
K: Yes. So they don't mind being criticized in general terms. But on specific terms, they get so defensive.
C: Don't criticize any person in a specific situation.
K: You have to do that very carefully, in a discreet way. We have to prudently, carefully point out or criticize in a roundabout way.

The other way is to have initially certain kinds of rapport. You have to go to Ginza together. You have to have a cup of sake together on a buddy-buddy basis. With the help of alcoholic beverage, with the help of building up initial rapport, there is a basis, a room for accepting any kind of criticism or critique with less defensiveness.

The way we approach criticism must be differentiated from your direct approach.

C: You have to do it the Japanese way.

K: Yes. Some people do not want to lose face. But some people do welcome criticism. The younger people who are more aggressive and competing as managers are now open-minded. They just accept whatever you say, even though it might hurt. It *is* changing. But I think we have to be more prudent and discreet, and be careful in pointing out, in bringing out the confrontation. But we do that, too.

C: So your clients do appreciate the inputs given in this manner, even though the feedback may disturb the status quo and may disturb the ongoing direction.

UNDERSTANDING JAPANESE MANAGEMENT—A CAUTION:

K: Yes. One other thing, as a footnote, that is important. I think there are new myths, or new misunderstandings about the nature and quality of Japanese management—seniority management, permanent employment and such things. Westerners seem to have understood certain words which might describe *partially* the truths and validity of Japanese managerial behavior. But you have to be very careful not to make a quick and hasty generalization.

For instance, if you say about Japanese management that they have permanent employment, this is a half truth. The people who are covered by permanent employment at such workplaces are only 25 percent of the workforce—in the large established organizations. Even the large organizations do have a system of a safety valve, like temporary workers, or the part-time or seasonal workers. You can easily fire them, or hire them again. So that is one precaution.

It is also misleading to say that Japanese wages are based on seniority only. This is only partly so. According to Ministry of Labor research, 40 percent of the wages in Japanese organizations are now determined by performance, skills, by what you have done—60 percent of the wages are still determined by the education, what school you went to, seniority, and other factors.

C: And which way is it moving? Toward performance?
K: Yes, toward performance.
C: Is that partly because of the influence of the many Japanese who are traveling abroad?
K: That is one answer. If you are to compete in the international market, there is no other choice but to conform to an international law or principle of management.

HOW CAN WE LEARN FROM THE JAPANESE?
C: I want to ask this question. In what way can Japanese management scholars or consultants be of help to us Americans?
K: (Laughter) That's a very difficult question.
C: Let me just say this: I ask this question, having just come from Bangkok, Singapore, Kuala Lumpur and Hong Kong, and having spent time in Tokyo now in two visits, and I am very impressed both with that I have seen here in Tokyo and in those countries in terms of the result—the visible results of Japanese management. They are exciting, dynamic results — of marketing, of advertising, of acceptance of Japanese products which are in place there. I see success here. Now I don't want to overdo it, but I come from America where right now, at least,

we are somewhat on the decline. So I say to myself, there is some wisdom here. There is some good experience here. There is some success here. How can we benefit? Because I want to help my own clients in America, and my American colleagues. I want to pass the word along.

K: There are three or four areas that we will be able to contribute to your success in the U.S. based on our experience here in Japan domestically, and abroad in the U.S., in the Southeast Asian countries and, to some extent, in Europe. I could give a couple of examples in the U.S.

For instance, Kyoto Ceramic employs about 1,000 people in San Diego. This is an electronic component manufacturer. They have plants not only here but also in the U.S. When they first went to San Diego they had difficulty—to their surprise. They had almost shockingly high absenteeism. Turnover was more than 86 percent a year. They were employing mostly blue collar workers—Spanish speaking blue collar workers—and they thought that they might be able to apply our Japanese group oriented/egalitarian approaches. They tried to make no differentiation between blue collar or white collar workers as managers. They tried to see the people as working as a team. At first they employed the "honor employee" system. Workers who had not been absent from the plant for six months (unless they had a good reason) were awarded a special status called "honor employee." An honor employee will never be fired by the foreman. The termination of his employment must be the decision of the vice-president. So there was job security. They are not immediately fired. And honor employees were also given priority in taking their vacations at the time they wanted it. Those privileges.

Also, Japanese people like pep talks. In the morning, also, they do the exercises.

C: Calisthenics.

K: Yes. Together, blue collar and white collar. And also in the morning singing the company song. They used all these Japanese approaches, as experiments. The singing of the company song, the exercises and the pep talks are quite common in Japan.

They were able to reduce the turnover somewhere in the neighborhood of 30 percent.

LAY-OFFS:

K: Another example is a case where I have been helping personally: Kikkoman Soy Sauce, in Wisconsin, U.S.A. Now, Kikkoman pledged to the employees that lay-offs will be very, very last resort. If the business goes down, unfortunately, then we will consult with you and we would like to ask your advice, your ideas. With your consultation—with the employees' approval, we'd like to—if it is OK—we'd like to decrease the wage basis so that we can at least guarantee—share— the hard, difficult times without firing anybody. That's one approach.

EGALITARIAN APPROACHES:

K: In the case of YKK, the largest Japanese-owned company in Atlanta, they have black managers, with white people reporting to them. Our egalitarian approaches have been particularly accepted by underprivileged people—frankly speaking—blue collar people, or minority people. Initially, they are puzzled and they don't like the idea, but as we go on, they accept our ways.

So far there are about ten Japan-based companies in the U.S. which have more than 1,000 employees. It is so limited. If you employ more than 1,000 or 10,000, then I don't think this kind of approach would turn out to be a panacea. That is one thing.

SMALL, AUTONOMOUS GROUP EMPHASIS AND THE SUGGESTION SYSTEM:

K: The second thing that has to do with American management is our emphasis on the small, autonomous group. QC (Quality Control) Circles are one example. Or the suggestion system group. Or the industrial-engineeing study group. Or work improvement group. The emphasis on the small group. I think that you might be able to learn a bit from our own experience because in the huge organization the basis is the small organization. We try to give emphasis to the autonomous approaches of each individual group. Small groups are usually encouraged to come up with ideas, suggestions, and even though we don't pay enough for the suggestion as you do—for instance, you pay about 10 percent of the savings in the American suggestion system and we pay only 1 percent or less than 1 percent — we give group incentives for those kinds of groups which are successful in the ideas. For instance, in the best case—they can go to the U.S. or to Europe.

C: A group trip? The whole group will go together?

K: Yes. Also, in minor cases they can come up from the southern part of Japan to Tokyo for five-day meetings and sight-seeing, etc. Group incentive is great. We also used to think those who bathe together can work together better.

C: Have any group awards of that nature been used in the U.S. yet?

K: Yes. I can give you a copy of my presentation "The Comparative Analysis of the Suggestion System of U.S.A. and Japan." Also I can give you the voiced part of the videotape which has been recently recorded. We have gone into the details about the suggestion systems. Also, the emphasis on the small group can be more amply explained in the materials and the tape which I am going to give you.

C: Good. Thank you. So, essentially, two approaches that we could learn are, first, the egalitarian approach and secondly, an emphasis on small, autonomous groups. As you know, QC Circles are now somewhat the rage in the States. I have been informed that only about 5 percent of the companies in Japan utilize QC Circles. In speaking of small, autonomous groups, were you also including QC Circles?

K: I don't have any specific figures now, but my paper will provide you with an analysis of the Japanese QC and small group approaches. I think the figure is more than 5 percent. And also, the QC Circle is nothing but the tip of the iceberg, because even though they do not call them QC Circles, there are many small group activities always going on.

WORK CLUSTERS:

K: For instance, in the formal organization, if you go to any company's plants, you would be surprised to find out that the different ways of assembling, the work arrangement—the layout is quite different. We usually have this kind of cluster type of approach (draws it). This is the manager (draws) and the people here, so this is how we usually arrange the desks. Whereas in the U.S., the manager is watching from behind, or the executive manager has a small individual office. In the cluster approach in Japan you can have very good communication.

C: Where the manager is really included within the people arrangement. That is the egalitarian notion you were talking about.

K: Yes. He should be a part of the team.

MORNING STAFF MEETINGS:

K: And usually in the morning—if you go to any department store or any company—each group has its own morning staff meeting.

C: How long is the meeting?

K: Five or ten minutes. What are the priorities we should emphasize? We don't make it a big affair — but this is a typical built-in Japanese system.

C: Department stores, plants, banks. A daily occurrence. Does it have a name, that meeting?

K: Morning courtesy, morning bow, morning pep-talk. Cho-ray. Cho = morning; ray = bowing.

C: Does that come from a long tradition, historically?

K: Yes. I don't know when it started. It is a part of *us*. We start the day in this fashion.

SUGGESTIONS:

C: You were saying earlier that QC Circles are really only the tip of the iceberg. This interests me very much. For instance, let's return to "suggestions" for a moment. I saw in the Asahi Evening News just the other night that the Toyota Motor Company received over 286,000 suggestions from over 46,000 employees within a year. Now, I find that a stupendous statement of openness to suggestions. Can you comment on that?

K: (Smiling) This is not to knock the suggestion system. But sometimes employees are *forced* to come up with suggestions. In a typical Japanese approach in the performance rating, one of the important things is to find out how many suggestions the individual has come up with. When I was a member of one of the companies, we just used to kid ourselves. If you made any suggestion, you would bring it to the personnel manager, or the Suggestion Box or the suggestion processing bureau, and they usually gave you a kind of token gift for the suggestion — a little handkerchief or soap. So when we would run out of soap, we'd say, "Let's make some suggestions!"

C: So qualitatively, suggestions are not always good.

K: Qualitatively, they are not to be desired. But sometimes we are forced to make suggestions. We have an obsession with suggestions.

But joking aside, this is the other side of the suggestion system. There are very, very good suggestions. They are not only encouraged, but there is a campaign — usually once a year — "suggestion month" — "month of suggestion." And also group competition. Section 1 is coming up with suggestion 500; why don't we in Section 2 do that, too. Small goup competition for suggestions is very effective.

C: How are those suggestions listened to?

K: There are many channels for processing suggestions. But usually they are accepted by the Suggestions Bureau or the Processing Office or through the managers. There are three major channels. One is to go through the managers or supervisors. The second one is to bring it directly to the Suggestions Office, and the third one is the Personnel, Human Resources Office.

REWARDS FOR SUGGESTIONS:

K: Usually employees are notified of the receipt of suggestions. And they (the suggestions) will be processed and evaluated according to the merit, the savings possible and the result. Then there is a little award ceremony — usually once a month — when they are notified that they got the suggestion rank A or rank B or rank C.

C: There is a whole suggestion system.

K: We imported this system from your country.

C: Is that right? (Laughter). And then did a better job.

K: (Laughter) We imported QC system from Dr. Deming. We made a creative misunderstanding and modified the whole system. We combined your quality control with personal touches.

C: Japanese touches.

K: We quoted your PERT, your CRM system, you know, the schedule system process chart. We added the group approaches, the human touches.

JAPAN AS NUMBER ONE: (VOGEL)

C: We have previously talked about Vogel's *Japan as Number 1*. As you know, he is very, very optimistic and laudatory. Before I ask you "Do you agree with it," let me ask you about the Japanese reaction to that book.

K: Yes. This book sold close to 400,000 copies in translation (to Japanese) and, if I am not mistaken, I think his book sold in the U.S. 36,000 copies. So we sold ten times more than the original book.

C: That in itself is a statement, isn't it?

K: I had a chance to sit with Dr. Vogel in the seminar sponsored by the Japan Society in New York last year. This was immediately before his book came out. He said he was preparing for his book to be published. I asked what's the name. He said, "Japan as Number 1." I said to Dr. Vogel that a certain Japanese newspaper may misunderstand and title the book Japan *Is* Number 1. The Japanese people also have become complacent.

Because of their economic success, because of the growth of the GNP (before the first oil crisis in 1974), because of the tremendous growth economically, they also haven't been able to recover from the damage — the loss of face and self-confidence which we suffered because of the defeat in the last war (World War II). I think this book, in a way, is kind of an endorsement, and gives encouragement from the Japanese people's hangover from the previous days, their inferiority. I think they are now very much encouraged by this book. We are now endorsed and approved by the Harvard professor. We seem to have come up a long way from the postwar devastation.

THE JAPANESE LEARNING STYLE:

K: One of the important things is that he has, for the first time, pointed out to the American people our way of learning something. I think that previous Japanologists have almost never pointed out one of the important things that we think is quite natural. When we want to do something, we just try to learn and absorb all the possible answers, alternatives and developments not only in Japan, but in Europe, in developing countries and in the U.S. Then, by combining and by evaluating the best of all this, we try to come up with the optimum combinations which are available.

So that is one of the keys to explain the success of Japan.

For instance, we are very sophisticated copycats. I have accompanied many executives, many union people going abroad to study — groups of course. All top executives of chain stores, for instance, make two or three trips a year to Europe or to the U.S., I think.

C: To do what?

K: To learn something. To get something new.

C: Are you saying, then, that one of the secrets — and it is a point that Vogel does bring out — one of the secrets of Japanese success has to do with their desire, their urge to get the best . . .

K: . . . to collect information from all parts of the world.

C: That is, they don't exclude. They are *looking* for information. They are reaching out for it. And then they will put it together here, in their own way.

CREATIVE OPTIMIZATION:

K: Yes. With our own personal touch, in combination. For instance, you know our typical Japanese dish, tempura. It originated from the Jesuit fathers and brothers who came to Japan close to 500 years ago. They had been eating meat all this time. But during those days, because of Buddhist influences, no Japanese were allowed to eat any meat — any animals with four legs. So the story says, the Catholic brothers tried to cook the fritter (fried) type of food, still using the animal type of oil. They couldn't find any animal oil here, but they found the vegetable type of oil which is milder, and they fried the vegetables and fish in it. So this is the origin of tempura. So this kind of "creative optimization" or "creative misunderstanding" of the best things in the world is the name of the game here, I think. And so Vogel is correct in pointing that out for the first time.

K: If any Japanese manager wants to develop a new product, he likes to find out all the possible seeds — instead of the *needs,* here.

C: Seeds?

K: Seeds-oriented. Try to find a good seed rather than try to identify the needs here. For instance, the transistor —when the former chairman of Sony saw the article in Fortune magazine about the transistor, he imported it. I have been speaking over and over again of the obsession; the urge to absorb is quite high and intensified here.

C: Does this relate to the fact that in every bookstore I have gone into here in Tokyo, there are many, many Japanese people standing and reading or browsing? Kinokuniya is a five-storied bookstore, larger, perhaps than any other I have ever seen. And other bookstores, they're crowded. Is this part of that same obsession?

K: Yes.

OBSESSION FOR LEARNING:

C: Obsession for learning!

K: Just as we have Jewish mothers, Japanese-Jewish mothers, constantly nagging you to study. This explains why Japan is Number 2 with regard to the percentage of people who go to higher educational institutions. We have about 2.5 million college students. We have 1,036 colleges, including junior colleges and universities, second only to the U.S. And we have fewer dropouts. A college degree in the postwar period is hardly anything at all.

Before the war, in the early '30s, the French poet Jean Cocteau visited Japan, and when he came to Yokohama by ship what struck him most, at first sight, was that he saw a beggar — dirty — reading a newspaper.

C: Taking in information.

K: Yes.

OD CONCEPTS: Win-Win in Japanese Management

C: I want to ask you just a few questions about two OD concepts. I want to mention these concepts and then turn them around and see if we can look at them from the Japanese view. The first is the "win-win" concept. That is a behavioral science concept that we are often trying to teach managers. We know there is a good deal of competitiveness within organizations and we are trying to say to managers, "If you will change your methods slightly, and see to it that the other person wins, also, that may be beneficial to you." Now I want to come back to *nemawashi* — or the *ringi* process — we mentioned *nemawashi* earlier, with a built-in, win-win result; and in which there is nearly endless discussion on an informal basis — am I right?

K. Yes.

C: And in which there will be an effort to establish a workable, implementable consensus. Now, is this valued because it *is* a win-win process?

K: I think so. Yes.

C: I take it that you didn't come in with that notion of win-win; you didn't start with that.

K: We try to not win-lose. Yes: win-win. Everyone is supposed to win the game. Yes. You have given us a good insight.

C: As you know, I come to Japan fresh, with my own concepts, and I have read some, and we have talked a little about these decision-making processes — and problem solving — and I say: "That's interesting. That's win-win!"

K: I also have to point out, that our win-win is not to make a win-win, but a partial win-win. Sometimes in the U.S., in the win-lose, if the winner is a really brilliant guy, has an insight, has power, and is benefited by the circumstances, he might have incentive to win; whereas in Japan (we find) the win-win, consensus building, sometimes partial or shared win-win, poor win-win, or the unsatisfactory win-win.

C: So you see this as a negative aspect.

K: Yes.

And also I have to add that Dr. Vogel point out in his book, the important thing is that in Japan, because they encourage the middle management to speak up, Japanese middle management people have real power there. This is the power house and the engine room of Japanese management, particularly in large organizations. So they encourage the people with new ideas, new suggestions, new things. Win-win, yes. The important people are the middle management, not top management. So middle management people, even though they may not enjoy the highest status of an American president, can at least find their satisfaction in materializing their potentials in proposing good alternatives for the management. (Of course) sometimes top management make a hint or suggestion. This is also covered by Dr. Vogel.

OD CONCEPTS: Collaboration and Competition
C: Now, one other concept from our own behavioral sciences. As you know, *JABS* (Journal of Applied Behavior Sciences)* had a special issue several years ago on "Collaboration." The collaborative spirit seems to be prominent in Japanese management, and. . .
K: I think we have been practicing what *JABS* has been preaching.
C: What I wanted to ask you is: Is it a conscious force? Or does it grow out of the culture?
K: It is a concious effort.
C: I am intrigued. Can you describe this?
K: Sometimes we get too much annoyed by the preaching, or the conscious/unconscious of the importance of collaboration. We are fed up with collaborativeness. We can go to this extreme.
C: Well, that's interesting.

Let me test another notion related to this, Maurie. As I see it, there are often consortia of Japanese industries which undertake large construction projects, for instance. Is this another example of the natural proclivity toward collaboration? Here in Japan I find collaboration on a large scale that I don't find in the U.S.
K: There is collaboration between the government and the private sector. Sometimes this is misunderstood as mutual over-

* *Professor Kobayashi is an International Consulting Editor of the Journal of Applied Behavioral Sciences, published by the NTL Institute of Applied Behavioral Science, Washington, D.C.*

dependence by the private and public sectors.

C: That the private sector is really stronger than we might give credit for in terms of its economic responsibilities?

K: Yes. There is a subtle formal and informal cooperation between the government and the private sector. . . . I have to also hasten to add that if you are a member of us — or a member of this group — then you are accepted and you are expected to collaborate very fiercely; but if you are not a part of or a member of this group, then — shall we say — then you have to fight fiercely. This is not a dichotomy. This seemingly contradictory behavior is quite important. If you are a member of the Mitsui group — Mitsui helps each other. But if you are with the Mitsubishi group, and you are going to go to Singapore or any other country, Mitsui and Mitsubishi (trading companies) work very fiercely, for instance, to get the contract for a certain project.

C: So they compete with each other. So the collaboration is within spheres.

K: Within spheres!

C: There are different planets.

K: We and they.

C: So the competition is there.

K: Yes. Group against group.

C: To the benefit of the larger group, which is the Japanese . . . government? People? Emperor? Is there an appreciation of that? After all, though you compete, whoever gets the contract, it will still be a Japanese achievement. Is that it?

K: I am not as clear about that. Our selfishness is a group selfishness. Enlightened group selfishness. We are Japanese, and that is the common denominator between two competing groups. It is quite mistaken that we don't compete.

C: Does the Japanese Overseas Enterprise Association — remember, I visited them in Singapore through your assistance

— play a mediating role here in this competition? I notice there is an effort to train Japanese people abroad to help them become acculturated to the overseas countries they are working in.

K: Not mediation yet. Their primary duty so far as been to develop and train the people who will be sent abroad, especially as managers. Because we came to the international scene sometimes uninvited; sometimes a late comer. The Japanese Overseas Enterprises Association is composed of the many leading industrialists so there is also collaboration and competition there. They do compete, but they also collaborate.

LEARNING FROM WESTERN MANAGEMENT: Drucker and Others —

C: One thing I like, Maurie, is that you are willing to be critical, to look at the subtle differences that exist, that you are not taking a flat position one way or the other. I want to see if I can chase down your ideas about many of the management ideas and concepts that have come from modern, Western management. As I understand it, there is a flow of books and journal articles from the West that comes here, that perhaps more readily receive attention here in Japan than in the U.S.

K: Yes. Peter Drucker's book "The Practice of Management" sold more than 2½ million copies here in the '50s and '60s.

C: How do you account for that? Why did that happen?

K: Right after the end of the war (World War II), we thought we were still losing. We lost the war. We did not want to go into military power again, so the only possible way for a peaceful survival was to exert our efforts in the area of economics, as commerce merchants or producing the goods. We thought at that time that American productivity was so high, America was the leading power — economically and politically — the American system seemed to be functioning quite smoothly and favorably, so we thought that there might be some secret that we had not found in the Japanese environment. So that was one urge or stimulus to try to learn what seems to be behind America's great economic power. And then Peter Drucker very succinctly, realistically and dynamically described American management practices. So this was kind of a reflection of the times of the late '50s and early '60s. We wanted to find out, shall we say, the new common languages for management.

C: Those two million people — over two million who bought the book — were they mostly managers?

K: Managers and junior managers. The younger people, yes.

C: That means they bought the book and took it home and read it.

K: Yes, and tried to apply what is in it.

OD — ORGANIZATION DEVELOPMENT:

C: Is the concept of organization behavior accepted as such? Does one talk in Japan of "organization behavior" or "organization development?" Is either term familiar here?

K: Yes. We use OD . . . sometimes cynically. I think OD is quite misunderstood here. Let me find my article with Warner Burke about the history of OD here. OD in Japan is accepted, for somewhat different reasons. OD also in Japan created some disturbance when it came into the Japanese market because we thought we had enjoyed postwar tremendous growth. About 15 years ago there was a certain area that wasn't successful — management. We thought there was something wrong with our management, something wrong with the system; in order to find out, there was OD. Organization Development or Renaissance seemed not to be alien to us because of some of its basic concepts — there is some affinity.

C: What was it that you found wrong that you wanted to

correct?

K: One was the small groups and autonomous groups. They had been successfully launched; then, it seems they had gone into a deadlock, a plateau. That's one reason. Also, we observed some of the bureaucratic rigidities mushrooming again in Japanese organizations. We thought we eliminated them right after the war when everything had been destroyed. The red tape disease seemed to be one of the symptoms. And also we had to identify the problem of the beginning of overseas Japanese direct investment. We thought it had something to do with the cross-cultural differences. We were able to transplant our management to the different heterogeneous organizations abroad.

We tried, also, to import management by objectives, but it didn't seem to function. I think at that time we wanted to seek some new alternatives to help us solve various kinds of human resources problems. So OD is accepted in Japan, and sometimes very fanatically.

C: Now, so that the readers of this would have the same thing in mind that you have when you speak of OD, can you briefly indicate what OD involves in the way you are using it?

K: Our OD effort has primarily, centered around the courses related to training. In my perception OD is not simply for the training. There are many approaches. Training, education, trying to change the personnel — that's one area. Technological intervention is one area. Institutional intervention is one area. In Japan, I think OD is now regarded by most people as kind of a sophisticated form of training. People think that by training, or re-training, using various kinds of OD methods, they will be able to change the whole organization and system. We are still obsessed with training. Other interventions, other systems for the planned changes are not used as much.

C: So that is one criticism you are making of OD here.

K: Yes.

C: Do you have any other thoughts about OD in Japan now?

K: Another thing, before the oil crisis, we were more attracted by the love and trust approach. After the oil crisis we found suddenly that the world was not necessarily bound by rosy flowers and fragrance, but cold chilly power. For the past five years, our OD effort has been more attracted to the power analysis, or power theory, or power perceptions. This is not necessarily a 100 percent departure from the previous model — it is an area our OD had neglected.

C: Are you at all speaking of the virtues of shared power?

K: Machiavellian, adversary or authoritarian relations — we found ourselves in the realistic world, that if we just preach this kind of collaborative effort, the managers and executives, they complain. They say — particularly recently — that this OD and Behavioral Science is nothing but a sissy, unrealistic and idealistic (proposal). They are suffering.

And also, in the past five or six years, we have matured in OD I believe. We used to think of one alternative, one theory, one model as the omnipotent. For instance, everybody thinks Managerial Grid is an overall cure (Blake and Mouton). Those proponents of Grid believe that it can solve all their problems. And then up comes Transaction Analysis. Everybody says that TA is a panacea. And then comes up Herzberg's Job Enrichment. Because we have been absorbing, absorbing, absorbing and those who introduce or transplant the system think that this can solve all the problems. And now, realistically we have found out unless we take a situational approach, we will never ever be able to solve the problem by one, "the," method. Maybe LIFO (Life Orientation Method) can be used for an initial period; and this plant may be helped by "agreement management," and this plant may need some TA . . . And so, by studying them and comparing these imported approaches, plus our original Japanese approaches, and by matching these approaches — these interventions —with the actual situations, we will be able to come up with optimal blending of these methods.

C: Let me comment. From what you have said, there is an interest in reaching out for American concepts whether they are Herzberg, Blake and Mouton's Grid, Transaction Analysis or LIFO—you will give all these things a try, and place a great deal of faith in them, and attempt to work them out. Now you have reached a new point of maturity where you want to combine and take the best of those and tie them in with situations, the actual conditions that you are facing . . .

K: Plus re-analyzing what is typically Japanese.

C: . . . your own cultural demands.

K: Yes. And also, finally, Japanese OD clarifies Japanese values as differentiated from Western values, Japanese group norms, and Japanese ways of moving the organization.

C: I wonder if the theme of our interview is not an effort by an American coming to Japan to see what we can borrow from you. Everyone of these management ideas you have mentioned are American, things like LIFO, Job Enrichment, Grid. You have said that the Japanese are willing to go to all parts of the world for ideas, and then they will attempt to integrate them into their own environment. Now Americans are coming here to learn.

K: And also another realization recently is that when the Japanese economically were third or fourth or fifth, we had some target to catch up with the Germans, to catch up with the U.S. Now we have more or less caught up as far as economics is concerned. We have no master to learn from now. So we have to come up with our own ideas. So the days of creative misunderstanding, creative modification seem to be gone.

So this is a very difficult period, but very challenging. We have to try to find out the merits of different systems, and try to seek the training systems and approaches from abroad. But also, we have to make a deeper analysis of what we have here. And also, we have to make our own interventions. So by combining Western thought and Japanese systems and values we can apply these to new situations.

Marketing in Japan: How to Sell in Japan Effectively

Research: The Key to Success

The adage "a little learning is a dangerous thing" is most apt in the context of marketing in Japan. Often with only surface knowledge of the requirements of the market, many foreign entrepreneurs have tried and failed to successfully sell their products here. Frequently they blame their failure on the country's exceedingly complex distribution channels (as if the system were established to preclude foreign participants) or on "protectionist" government policies. Barriers to effective marketing in Japan, however, are created not so much by "closed doors" as they are by closed minds. People with gaps in their knowledge who are self-appointed "experts" claim that the Japanese market is inaccessible. But such a charge is proven groundless when a marketer, backed by adequate research, tries to tap the great potential that the Japanese market offers.

Building from the rubble that was the result of World War

II, Japan has managed to restructure its devastated economy. Today the country is the world's leading shipbuilder and producer of consumer electronic goods and automobiles, to name only a few successes. (In 1979 Japan produced 10 million cars, the largest number that any nation has ever built in a single year.) But the country's new prosperity has not been at the cost of foreign participation. In fact, it is because of its economic success and the resulting prosperity that Japan has become an increasingly attractive market for foreign businessmen.

The most lucrative features of the Japanese market are its size and wealth. Crowded on the islands that make up Japan (the total land area of which is only 1/25 that of the United States) live over 118.5 million people. They speak the same language, are highly literate (over 99 percent of the population can read and write—the highest literacy rate in the world) and earn a per capita income equal to approximately US$10,000. Annual total savings per household about matches that figure. But the Japanese market is not limited to households; corporations here are well known to be big spenders. Company expense accounts and other perks annually reflect an estimated one percent of the nation's GNP.

A country endowed with few natural resources, Japan has long been an important market for foreign producers of industrial raw materials and foodstuffs. It has also been an important consumer market. Entrepreneurs from abroad who are customer-oriented and who are determined to identify and meet the needs and desires of the market have found ample opportunity to sell their wares in Japan. Coca-Cola and Pepsi Cola control a large segment of the Japanese soft drink industry. Twining and Lipton enjoy major shares of the Japanese tea market, and Johnnie Walker successfully competes with Japan's domestic producers of whiskey.

Just how well foreign enterprises have penetrated the market is illustrated in this scenario of a typical Japanese businessman's morning. Waking to an alarm that uses foreign-assembled semiconductor chips, the Japanese businessman starts his breakfast with Maxwell or Nestle coffee. He may have a slice of bread that was baked under the guidance of a French technician and that uses flour from Portland, Oregon. For toast, he may use butter from New Zealand and strawberry jam produced in England. Donning a suit made from imported Australian wool, he tries to make a subtle distinction in class by putting on a Gucci tie and Bally shoes. (Career women are equally conscious about the way they look; they add a touch of class by wearing the popular Yves Saint Laurent, Pierre Cardin, or Calvin Klein designs.)

Almost any quality product that is reasonably priced (and even those that are not reasonably priced) can be successfully marketed in Japan. Office equipment, sporting goods, medical equipment, cosmetics, records, processed foods, musical equipment, farm machinery, and clothing are only some of the many kinds of foreign-made products holding major market shares in their respective fields in Japan. The common characteristics of the companies marketing these products is their willingness to research and identify the needs of Japanese consumers and adapt their products and methods of marketing accordingly. Ambitious foreign businessmen who have open minds and exert the extra effort will undoubtedly be handsomely rewarded.

It is said a shrewd businessman can sell refrigerators to Eskimos, not to refrigerate, but to insulate food from the freezing Arctic environment. In the same sense, a businessman interested in the Japanese market should not be discouraged by claims that it is "inaccessible." An entrepreneur has every chance for success in Japan provided he researches the requirements of the market and is able and willing to fill the need.

Distribution Channels

"Complex and fragmented." That is how Westerners, more often than not, describe distribution channels in Japan. Simple, straightforward channels with the smallest number of middlemen, they say, will best serve the interests of consumers.

Westerners who view Japan's distribution system as "archaic" and "inefficient" are not alone. Even some Japanese involved in the distribution sector are pushing for drastic changes. They want to "modernize" distribution by streamlining and eliminating some of the layers that separate producers and end users.

Certainly Japanese distribution channels are more complex than comparable channels in the United States. But as of late, the dominant view in Japan is that the system here fits the needs of demanding Japanese consumers. While furniture stores in the United States, for example, may take up to 10 weeks to deliver goods ordered at their showrooms, Japanese consumers would not stand for such long delays. In most cases, furniture ordered in Japan is delivered within a week. Because of consumer importance, manufacturers, wholesalers, and retailers alike are forced to carry somewhat excessive inventories; their respective distribution centers are scattered throughout Japan to enable them to make quick deliveries.

In any highly industrialized country, where the needs and desires of sophisticated consumers are constantly changing, marketers must "think small." In Japan, monolithic mass production and mass merchandizing have given way to a more "demassified approach," a movement observed on a global scale by Alvin Toffler and explained in his recent best-seller, *The Third Wave*. In view of such an approach, Japan's distribution

Flow Charts of Selected Distribution Channels in Japan

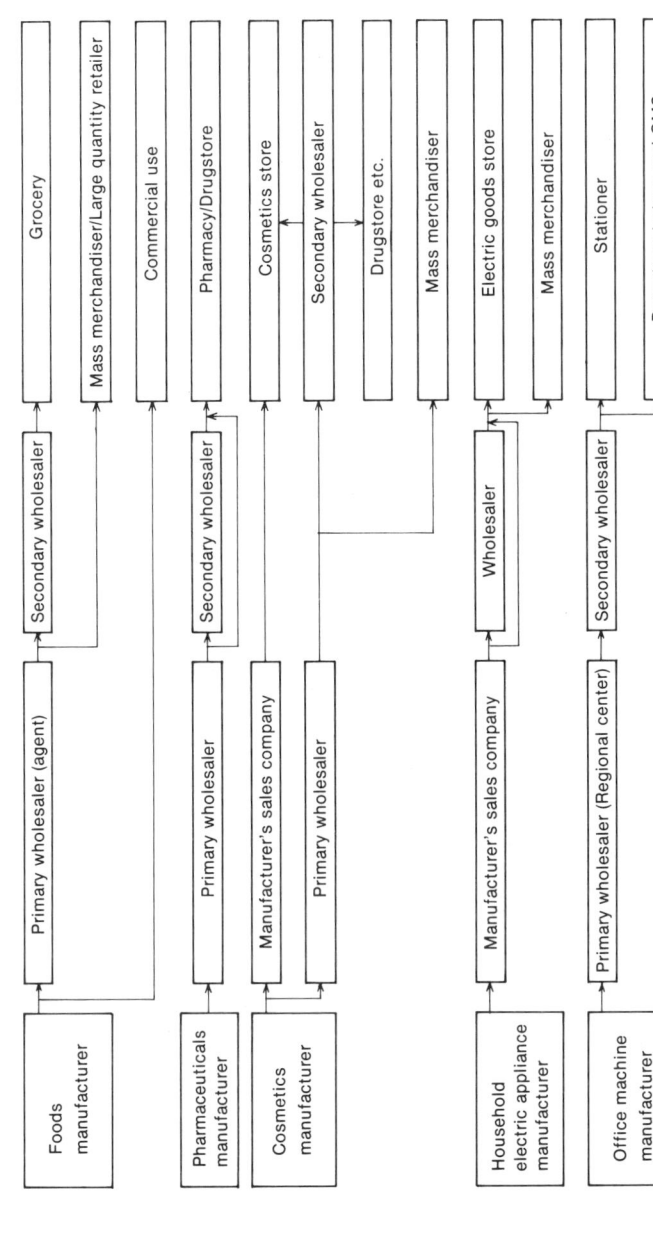

Source: *Marketing Oppotunities in Japan* (1978)

system cannot be simply regarded as "archaic" and "inefficient."

According to a report by Dentsu, Japan's largest advertisement agency, foreign businessmen typically characterize distribution channels in Japan as lengthy and diversified. In fact, however, distribution routes in Japan are neither particularly longer nor particularly more complex than those in Europe. Japan's distribution channels have traditionally been segregated by product type, giving rise to the development of many specialized marketing routes.

About 20 years ago, a book entitled *The Distribution Revolution* sensationalized the idea that wholesalers in Japan were a dying breed. Though the book was provocative and attracted a great deal of attention, the dire predictions it made have not materialized in the past two decades.

Wholesalers in Japan are alive and well, performing a variety of functions, such as purchasing, marketing, transportation, storage, financing, information gathering, production planning, risk management, and even management consulting. In other countries, many of those functions are reserved for manufacturers or retailers or both. Japanese wholesalers have been able to take on these functions and run efficient operations, often using computers to control sophisticated, semi-automated distribution centers.

In contrast to the relative stability in the wholesaling industry, the retailing industry in Japan changed remarkably in the past decade, and apparently it will continue to change. Large department stores in Japan have captured about 10 percent of domestic retail sales. But their strong market position has been overtaken by "supers," or general merchandise stores, which handle about 15 percent of retail sales. Self-service and convenience chain stores have also grown rapidly and together they have gained a 15 percent share of the market.

Daiei, the largest general merchandise store in Japan, with annual sales reaching 1.2 trillion yen (about 52 billion dollars), is now advancing into new areas of retailing and service. For example, it recently concluded an agreement with Au Printemps of France to open medium-sized prestige stores under the Au Printemps name. Daiei also concluded an agreement with K-Mart, a large U.S. retailer, to exchange merchandise and merchandising know-how. Daiei's interest in foreign merchandising know-how may have something to do with the fact that many foreign and Japanese entrepreneurs have successfully transplanted to Japan retailing concepts conceived overseas. The successes of franchise chain restaurants like McDonald's and convenience food stores like Seven-Eleven are two of many examples. Other foreign-born retailing concepts, like voluntary chain stores, co-ops and shopping centers, have also proven viable in Japan, though none are exactly like their foreign originals. One difference between foreign and Japanese shopping centers, for example, is the amount of space available for parking. Because of the low availability and high cost of land, Japan's largest shopping center has room for only 6,000 cars. That is considerably less space than what is available at sprawling U.S. regional shopping centers, where there is often room for more than 10,000 automobiles.

But what Japan lacks in space, she makes up for in ingenuity, as is seen in the rapid development of fabulous underground malls and arcades. Connected to the terminals of major train and subway lines, underground arcades, like Subnard in Tokyo and Hachibangai in Osaka, provide Japanese consumers with convenient, comfortable places to shop. Moreover, these underground malls usually consist of more than 200 stores, restaurants, and service facilities, making them much larger and more numerous than underground shopping centers found in other countries.

Many new kinds of mass-marketing retail concepts caught on during the period of Japan's rapid economic growth. As Japan's economy stabilized in the late 1970s, however, the growth of mass-marketing retailers decelerated.

Despite these and other changes that have taken place over the past 15 years in Japan's retail industry, independent retailers maintain a powerful market share—about 60 percent of total retail sales. They have been able to do so because they continue to provide personalized and elaborate customer services and because they continue to hold controlling interests in their own businesses. Independent retailers, however, are not without their own serious shortcomings, such as the want of management skills; small total capital investments, which limit the assortment of goods available to customers; and most important, higher selling prices. Because of these and other problems, independent retailers have begun to organize themselves in order to compete with mass retailers. Some have joined franchise or voluntary chains.

Another recent development in Japan's retail industry is the emergence of mail-order sales. Though the mail-order business in Japan is still in its infancy, some stores are already experiencing remarkable success, such as Takashimaya Department Store, which had mail-order sales totaling 25 billion yen in 1983. Foreign retailers like Quelle of West Germany and Sears Roebuck of the United States are also entering the mail-order business in this country. As an aside, it is interesting to note that America's Franklin Mint, a maker of novelty gifts marketed by mail-order, was the most profitable foreign enterprise in Japan in 1979 in terms of a capital investment percentage. Mail-order sales may well develop rapidly in the years ahead owing to ever increasing energy costs and rising wages in Japan.

Though less important in Japan than mail-order sales, door-to-door sales have had a considerable impact on the successful sales of certain products, such as cosmetics, automobiles, language tapes, and musical instruments. But like mail-order sales, future success of door-to-door sales is largely dependent upon whether or not production and labor costs (the costs of a salesman's visit) will continue to rise.

Distribution channels are the link between manufacturers and consumers. No crucial difference in the functions of such channels exists between Europe, America, and Japan. According to one marketing consultant, however, by the very fact that it is the sector directly connected with the final consumer in any product field, it is naturally affected by the social, cultural, and historical conditions peculiar to a country. To that extent, the customs and practices in the distribution of products can be quite different from one country to another, while basically fulfilling the same functions required for the delivery of products from manufacturers to consumers.

Understanding the "peculiarities" of Japan's distribution system, is a giant step toward penetrating one of the world's most promising, but demanding consumer markets.

Japanese Consumer Psychology

To successfully penetrate the steadily growing consumer market in Japan, exporters should be aware of some special traits of Japanese consumer psychology.

One of the most important of these traits is the fascination with *hakurai-hin,* or foreign-made products. Literally, *hakurai-hin* means "goods borne by ship." But the term has a connotation of goods from mysterious, faraway places. Companies that have successfully exploited the potential of the Japanese market have either knowingly or unknowingly responded to the Japanese consumer's desire for *hakurai-hin*. Johnnie Walker is a familiar brand name to all Japanese consumers because its maker has not forgotten to advertise that the origin of this fine Scotch whisky is in Great Britain. And importers of fancy sports cars are also fully aware of the importance of stressing that their products were designed and assembled abroad.

The *hakurai-hin* syndrome may also explain in part the wide acceptance of foreign name-brand merchandise. The popularity of "designer" jeans is just one example. Foreign designer jeans are no different from ordinary jeans. But because they have the brand name displayed on the hip pocket, they sell extremely well, despite their outrageously high prices.

Why are the Japanese attracted to *hakurai-hin?* Though there is no definitive answer to that question, Taku Ibuki, a respected marketing psychologist, suggests two major reasons. The first stems from the fact that Japanese society is polytheistic and therefore flexible in blending a wide variety of foreign beliefs with those that are indigenous. Such blending can be seen in the fact that the Japanese "celebrate" Christmas, but listen to the Buddhist temple bells on New Year's Eve and celebrate New Year's Day by visiting a nearby Shinto shrine. That tolerance, or perhaps more accurately, that wide acceptance of foreign concepts, seems to have paved the way for the acceptance and admiration of foreign goods.

The second reason Ibuki gives for the Japanese attraction to *hakurai-hin* has to do with the somewhat disguised, but deep-rooted sense of inferiority Japanese feel in their relationships with other industrialized countries. That sense of inferiority is derived in large part from the fact that Japan was a latecomer to the modern world. The theory is that because of their inferiority complex, the Japanese are eager to lay their hands on anything newly imported.

Whatever the reason, the fact remains that foreign-made goods, for the reason that they are foreign made, are attractive to the Japanese consumer—an important point for any marketer to keep in mind.

Another trait of Japanese consumer psychology is the strong desire for a better standard of living. In the postwar era, Japan has tirelessly worked to build an economy that produces one of the largest per capita GNPs and the highest wages in the world. But despite their economic success, most Japanese are dissatisfied with the quality of their lives. In 1978 an EC official reportedly said that "the Japanese are workaholics living in rabbit hutches." Though that remark brought official indignation, many Japanese would agree with the assessment. In a survey taken by the Ministry of Construction's Housing Bureau, 38.9 percent of all households had "complaints about housing." Of those complaints, "homes being too small" ranked first. After years of sacrifice and hard work, Japanese are looking to reap the rewards of prosperity. Thus, emphasis is being placed on creating a better living environment for all, for example, by building more public parks and better facilities for the aged and handicapped. Prosperity has also led to a greater demand for leisure time.

The desire for a taste of "the good life" has created new opportunities for foreign manufacturers as the attention now being payed to the cultural and aesthetic side of living has given rise to new markets and a greater demand for all sorts of quality goods. Golf equipment, furniture, art work, clothing, food and beverages, and household items, such as crystal glasses and silver tableware, are only a few examples.

Finally, perhaps one of the most striking traits of the average Japanese consumer is his or her "schizophrenic" pattern of buying. While the Japanese are eager to buy high-priced, quality imports, they are just as eager to find a bargain.

Unlike Japan's socially stratified prewar society, class distinctions are minimal in Japan today. According to a survey taken by the Prime Minister's Office in 1981, 89 percent of the Japanese people believe they belong to the middle class. In fact, income distribution statistics support that notion. Since most Japanese consider themselves to be somewhere between the upper class and the lower class, their buying habits tend to be rather irregular. That is to say, they neither solely buy high-quality goods nor solely buy cheap, low-quality goods. Rather, they buy a mixture. Thus, for example, the Japanese purchase high-quality imported wine when entertaining guest, and cheaper wines for everyday use.

All these traits have important implications for marketers. Those who pay close attention to these and other patterns of Japanese consumer behavior and incorporate their observations into their marketing strategies will undoubtedly be successful.

Packaging in Japan

"The package is the silent salesman," said James Pilditch, one of the pioneers of modern packaging, a persuasive consumer marketing technique. The comment is more pertinent than ever before, especially in the case of Japan. Silent though it may be, packaging works well to attract the attention of demanding Japanese consumers, and serves as an effective tool for exploiting the great potential of the Japanese market.

In Japan, the importance of packaging is not something new, though modern packing technology and the country's sophisticated packaging industry are definitely the products of postwar economic development. For more than ten centuries, the Japanese have attached aesthetic value to the way things are packed. They are great admirers of carefully constructed packages, which in this country hold just about anything, including food and money.

One item that illustrates the Japanese ardor for packaging is the *makunouchi bento,* a beautifully arranged box lunch found in all parts of Japan. The variety of foods found in the *makunouchi bento* is almost limitless. The boxes themselves are made of any number of materials, wood or craft paper being most common. The significance of the *makunouchi bento* is that it satisfies consumers by serving an appetizing lunch in a way that appeals to the Japanese sense of compartmentalized beauty. Moreover the box lunch, with its wide assortment of foods, at least partially satisfies individual tastes.

The *furoshiki,* or cloth bag, is another example of the Japanese concern for the way things are packaged. The *furoshiki* is a square cloth made of silk, cotton, or some other fabric, used to wrap and carry goods. The motif of the cloth is so ornate that it can also double as a scarf. Most households have a supply of a half dozen large ones for carrying bulky items, and small purple ones for wrapping contributions of money or gifts.

Some Packing Tips

In designing packaging that appeals to Japanese consumers, marketers should keep several important points in mind.

The first is that, as mentioned in a previous article, the Japanese are attracted to *hakurai-hin,* goods from mysterious, faraway places. Many marketers have taken advantage of that fact by designing packages that create a foreign image in the minds of Japanese consumers. Illustrations of castles or landscapes of distant lands on the packages of imported alchoholic beverages, for example, have worked well to create such an image.

A second point to keep in mind when designing packages for the Japanese market is that homes in Japan are generally small. Consideration must be given to space so that packages can be easily stored.

A third point to remember when deciding packaging design is that distribution channels are somewhat longer in Japan than they are in other countries. "Long distribution channels usually increase demand on the strength of the package," warns Dr. Vern Terpstra, professor of international marketing at the University of Michigan. Packages must be durable enough to protect the product until it reaches the shelf of a retail outlet.

Retailers in Japan are adamant about not accepting shipments with smeared packages or ripped containers. Rather than accept the goods at a discount price, in many cases they reject the shipment in its entirety.

Quality control goes hand in hand with the notion of designing durable packaging. Most Japanese companies have strict quality control programs, which include the packaging of their products. The care given to packaging according to the Committee for Manufactured Goods Import Measurer "partly derives from the fastidious nature of Japanese consumers." For whatever the reason, Japanese manufacturers maintain high standards for packaging; foreign manufacturers who wish to compete successfully in the Japanese marketplace are advised to do likewise.

A fourth area to be considered carefully when selecting or designing packaging for Japan are the climatic differences within the country. Except for Hokkaido, the main northernmost island, Japan suffers a very hot and humid rainy season (called *bai-u*) from early June to mid-July each year. Packaging must therefore protect against mildew and decomposition. In the winter, temperatures in the coldest regions drop to as low as 20°C below zero. In the warmest regions, temperatures never fall below 5°C.

It is also important to consider tastes and customs when deciding upon packaging for consumer goods. The following examples perhaps best illustrate the point.

Coffee in the eastern part of the United States is ordinarily packaged using blue or greenish colors to reflect the preference of customers in that region to drink strong, black coffee. In the western part of the United States, however, coffee is usually packaged in reddish colors to reflect the regions preference for weaker coffee with cream. In Japan coffee is most commonly packaged in gold and black. One American food company altered its coffee packages from red to black and gold and began a new promotional campaign. Within two months the company has increased its market share in Japan threefold.

Large-sized beer bottles in Japan are an example of how custom has influenced packaging. Whereas in other countries people take pleasure from having their own beer bottle and pouring their own beer, in Japan the custom is to drink collectively, with everyone using the same bottle and pouring drinks for everyone else. Rarely do the Japanese drink alone. Thus, beer-makers here offer a large-sized bottle that can accommodate a group of people.

Other Things to Keep in Mind

The first oil crisis shocked the Japanese people into the realization that there are limits to Earth's natural resources. Ever since, Japanese consumers have demanded conservation of materials used in packaging. The outcry has helped to do away with excessive and unnecessary packaging. Department stores and chain stores have been the leaders in simplifying extravagant and wasteful packaging.

To some extent the government regulates packaging and package labeling. Agricultural goods, for example, must meet certain government standards, as must electric products, and be marked accordingly.

There are no schools of packaging in Japan, as there are in other countries, but the Japanese packaging industry, related associations, consumer groups, and government agencies have worked toward improving packaging technology and methods. As a result, Japan's packaging industry has grown tremendously in the past decade. Today "Tokyo Pack," the country's largest packaging exhibition, annually attracts upwards of 120,000 people from 40 different countries.

Sophisticated packaging systems are, of course, available in Japan. In fact, many foreign producers find it more efficient to export their products in bulk and have their goods packaged here.

In any analysis of effective packaging for Japan, marketers should always be alert to changes in consumer habits and values as income rises and retailing becomes more sophisticated. The appropriate package of the future may be very different from what is being used today.

Accordingly, if foreign marketers can identify new trends and package their goods, they may very well be able to win a large share of the lucrative consumer market in Japan.

Japanese Management and Labor

(1)　Innocent Abroad

When discussing Japanese management and effectiveness, one must consider the weaknesses as well as the strengths of Japanese management abroad. There are 4 areas of weakness: language, racial understanding, religion, and lack of appreciation of socially stratified classes.

The Japanese have a deep-rooted difficulty in speaking a foreign language. This is probably partly because of a Zen-based distrust of clearly expressed thoughts or ideas. The Japanese do not believe in the validity of verbal expression. This is also somewhat related to a shame-bound culture where the concept of keeping interpersonal relations and saving face is important. Trial by error—needed when learning to speak a foreign language—has been more or less alien to the Japanese. Historically Japan is an insular, homogenous country. Until recent times the nation could survive without bothering with another language.

Lack of experience with internal racial tensions and problems is another drawback. Japan has experienced some discrimination problems and racial prejudice, but they don't compare to those in other countries. The Japanese naively tend to believe that those with the same skin color and hair will all act, think, and feel the same way. This causes them to ignore the sensitivities and feelings of others.

With few exceptions the Japanese are not a religious people in the Western sense of the word. Religion here is a family affair and based on tradition. While the Japanese have moral principles, they have usually no strong religious beliefs, are quite tolerant toward many religions and have secularized and assimilated them. Nor are they well-informed on other religions, which sometimes leads them to offend foreign sensibilities.

Social classes do exist in Japanese society but they are not rigid compared to those in the West. The boundaries, too, are vague. In the U.S., the trend is towards requiring an MBA degree in order to rise to a high management position. In Japan, for instance, even the high school students have more opportunity for vertical mobility. Will power or *jitsuryoku* also plays an important role. Inherent in the meaning of this word is the concept of competency in a particular business area and in interpersonal relations. At the same time, modesty is required. If you have *jitsuryoku,* then, you have a good chance of moving up in the world. When visiting many Japanese factories, it is difficult to determine who is the boss—everyone wears the same uniform and eats in the same cafeteria.

(2) Employee Relations and Personnel Practices

To understand the Japanese employment system, one still needs to fully appreciate the three important interlocking institutions, namely life-long employment, seniority-based wage structure and enterprise-union practices even though they are undergoing tremendous change.

As Prof. Katsumi Yakabe of Tokai University explains:

"The lifetime employment system stems from a tacit understanding between labor and management that an employee, once he joins a company, will stay with it until retirement age. The company, on its part, will not discharge the employee (except under extreme circumstances) until he reaches retirement age. The retirement age has traditionally been 55; but extensions of a few years have become a practice recently, and today 50 percent of all Japanese companies set their retirement age at 60.

"The system is thus quite different from those in the U.S. and Europe, where it is not necessarily the rule that an employee remain with the same company for 30 or 40 years. As such, the Japanese system exhibits both advantages and disadvantages not found in the West. On one hand it provides strong employment stability, while on the other this often leads to undesirable rigidity. The stability is generally felt to be more favorable to the employees, while the rigidity is a disadvantage for management, particularly in times of recession. Why then, we may ask, is management just as eager as labor to continue this type of employment system?

"The most obvious answer is that it serves as a guarantee against future labor shortages. This, however, is only a partial answer; the real reason lies much deeper. It has to do with the moral and sentimental relationship between employer and employee. This relationship, heretofore valued highly by both parties, is an integral part of the traditional Japanese economic world, and even of Japanese society in a much larger sense. Thanks to this system, the employee feels he can place his trust and reliance in the company, and at the same time, he has a heightened sense of participation and identity with the company.

"By the same token, the system's stability allows management to place its trust in the continuing service and cooperation of the employees, creating a sentiment closely akin to parental concern. The system also encourages each member to place high priority on the grooming of his successor.

"The system has, however, drastically reduced the flexibility of the labor market, creating a clear distinction between a mobile labor force and a permanent one. The latter group constitutes the nucleus of the labor force for industry, while the mobile labor force is considered only a secondary or tertiary force and even, under certain circumstances, an undesirable one until recently."

(3) Recent Trends and New Challenges

Coming back to the starting point of our analysis of Japanese management, it is now confronted with big challenges. It has to overcome, for example, the challenge of internationalization and augmented Japanese direct investment abroad, and thereby has to cope with the resultant managerial conflicts in overseas operations caused by cultural differences.

The Japanese manner of motivating people, in the words of a *Fortune* writer, is "to emphasize a highly personal approach to corporate life and encourage employees to participate in all aspects of company affairs."

The insular-minded, innately clannish or clubby Japanese, traditionally favoring paternalism and decision-making based on consensus have to face, for the first time in their business organizational history, the great challenge of adjusting their management and organization styles to the different cultural climates and social norms.

Likewise, domestically, Japanese organizations must tackle the various changing work ethics and values of the younger and better-educated workers, who are inclined toward more mobility, better quality of working life, more leisure and more self-actualization in a shorter time span.

But the amazing amoeba-like flexibility, adaptability and ingenuity of the Japanese organizational activity as demonstrated in previous critical times may be able to overcome these difficulties and 'hard times.'

So it seems to be the paramount responsibility for all of us to identify and redefine the real needs and goals of Japanese organizations so as to implement the necessary planned changes to meet with immediate and further requirements. Re-thinking along the lines of rediscovery of the strength of Japanese organizations and refining our awareness will thus contribute to better relations between Japan and other parts of the world.

Therefore, the key to working successfully with Japanese abroad boils down to broadmindedness on both sides, increasing areas of common knowledge among us, and communicating effectively. A closed mind and a defensive attitude must be eliminated.

Human Resources Development in Japan

Analysis of Its Wholistic Approach

One of the most popular topics for discussion among Japanese business management people recently — and perhaps to a certain extent in the U.S. — is the question of how and to what extent the Japanese way of managing people and organizations could be successfully applied to an American or non-Japanese work environment. This question has been asked increasingly, as Japanese direct investment in manufacturing industries abroad, particularly in the USA, has been accelerating for the past four years to cope with the protectionist trend in these markets.

According to the latest statistics, Japanese direct manufacturing investment made here last year grew by almost 70 percent above the previous year and reached approximately 6 billion dollars in total.

Sony has plants in San Diego and Atlanta, Mitsubishi Heavy Industries assembles MU-2 in Texas, Kikkoman produces soy sauce in Wisconsin and Nisshin Shokuhin manufactures "Cup-o'-Noodle" in New Jersey. And various surveys carried out by such organizations as Boston Consulting and Stanford University, as well as our own, have so far proved that manufacturers of Japanese origin have successfully adapted their Japanese managerial styles to the local environment. For instance, Kyocera's experiment with the 'Honor Employee System' in San Diego is a good example of this. The system, in a nutshell, provides that any employee will be exempt from punching a time-recorder if he or she has reported to work on time and has not been absent for six months in a row. And these "honor employees," even when they have trouble with their immediate supervisors, will not be fired without the approval of a vice president. Moreover, they will be given privileges and enjoy an advantageous position in case of transfers and promotions. A recent report shows that 250 workers, one third of the hourly-paid workers, are categorized as "honor employees."

Another example: Kikkoman in Wisconsin and many other companies pledge to their employees that the management will try their best not to lay off the employees, even in case of redundancy, but on the other hand, urges the employees to accept various alternatives, such as reduction of pay, temporary transfer, sharing of work, changing of work hours, etc., when business slows down. These practices are quite commonly observed in Japanese companies in times of recession and reduced backlogs. These and dozens of other examples of Japanese personnel practices, such as the self-disciplined, small, autonomous group method, 30-minute morning communication meetings, pep talks, bottom-up suggestion system meetings, and group competition bonus systems now seem to be widely, and more or less profitably, adopted by companies doing business in the USA.

But at the same time, there have been several examples where the workers do not necessarily respond to these Japanese management systems favorably, or where the system had to be abandoned because it took so much time for this kind of readjustment to be effectively implemented. There are also reports that indicate these programs frustrated both supervisors and union organizers. Therefore, it is an apppropriate time now for us to re-examine the Japanese work methods and value systems "on trial" or in the process of cross-fertilization.

As was suggested by some researchers earlier, one of the unique characteristics of Japanese organizational philosophy is its emphasis on groupness or "group-centeredness", in carrying out any functions or tasks. This is further supported by our egalitarian orientation. The Japanese are a group-oriented society. Take, for example, a group of tourists at a restaurant ordering breakfast. From the waiter's or waitress' point of view, taking orders form a group of Americans is no small matter. The individuals will be highly particular in tastes and desires. As I mentioned earlier, some will want coffee immediately, others later. Some will prefer orange juice, a few a large glass, the rest a small one, while others will want grapefruit juice.

Japanese behavior in the same situation will be quite the opposite. The waiter or waitress will have to consult the leader of the tourist group to receive a rather nonspecific order which miraculously applies to everyone. The leader will likely say, "Oh, whatever you think would be appropriate for this party," or "whatever the chef recommends," or whatever the leader decides for himself will somehow fit the entire group. Japanese like to call this simplicity and conformity of handling a group of tourists a "set-menu efficiency."

This mentality, which Professor Hiroshi Hazama has labeled "groupism," is probably the most distinguishing characteristic of the Japanese personality structure. It is never overlooked nor underestimated by the Japanese. The clearest example of how this mentality is manifested in organizational life is in its participant decision-making. As a rule, decisions are made more or less by consensus. In U.S. organizations this is usually the exception. Japanese, therefore, typically take more time in decision-making, but less time in implementation. For Americans the reverse appears to be the case.

But if you think that we do not take into consideration the individualistic desires and aspirations at all, you have been greatly misled. Differentiation, classification, and stratification do play important roles in Japanese business and other organizations alike, but very subtly. This is one of the seemingly egalitarian approaches.

For instance, quite often the employees here (regardless of their organizational ranks) are requested to wear company uniforms. Therefore, you can't distinguish a general manager from rank and file employees—like the Chinese People's Liberation Army from the outlook. But in one Japanese company in a southern California plant, the color and designs of the uniforms do reflect job classifications and titles.

Another illustration is found in the chairs they use in factory offices. The Japanese office managers have to make a delicate status distinction between managers and supervisors by differentiating the size and shape of the arms of the chairs.

One of the reasons why the Japanese like the preset assorted box lunches *(makunouchi bento)* can be explained in this context. In these multi-entre mini lunch boxes, you can find a bit of everything — seafood, vegetables, meats, sweets, rice, etc. Though they are prepared in uniform manner, people with different tastes are able to find at least one piece of food that they like.

Now let us explore a little bit more how our small-group oriented, clubbish, gregarious management patterns, partly developed by work, are applied to the American scene. I imagine that you have paid a visit at least once to Rocky Aoki's Benihana restaurant chain. There, unlike the ordinary American seating arrangement, you will find the "forced" seating system with complete strangers at the same table. This is based on our space and time-saving concept, developed to match the congested Japanese environment.

Other popular examples include our subcompact car, tiny portable videos, small computers — all of which are products designed to meet our limited living space. The whole culture is directed to what Schmacker succinctly termed the "small is beautiful" concept.

Since there is no choice other than living as harmoniously as possible in a narrow area, Japanese people have developed a variety of devices and wisdom for peaceful co-existence.

Now let's discuss the fourth important factor of Japanese organization: wisdom, which is now challenged in international context. This is the question of ambiguity aimed to achieve flexibility and harmony.

The person who has a very low tolerance for ambiguity would have a tough time in the Japanese organization. According to a study conducted by a Japanese student at International Christian University in Tokyo whom I quoted earlier, there are currently some 19 different ways for the Japanese to express "no" without actually saying the word "no." As a Japanese manager transplanted by Mitsubishi Corporation to one of its subsidiary plants in Texas expressed it, "I've had to learn to say 'no' instead of 'that's very difficult.' " The U.S. manner of being straightforward and "telling it like it is" sometimes causes conflict between boss and subordinate or among peers. Japanese see this kind of behavior as creating conditions for "losing face," an outcome they work to avoid. Keeping conditions ambiguous allows for face saving.

Japanese have many rules, regulations, and policies but as long as the interpretation of these norms and their implementation can be left vague, organization members can relate to one another with less strain and frustration. For the American this ambiguity often has the opposite effect. Interwoven closely with ambiguity is flexibility, another marked feature of the Japanese character. This behavioral characteristic is reflected in the continued popularity of the traditional kimono. This robe, typically cotton, requires no other garments for appropriate wear, is highly economical, and is convenient for either sex. Since it has wide front panels which overlap, the kimono is comfortable for a midriff of any circumference.

Examples within the Japanese organization include (a) the *sohmu* ("general affairs") department, a "permanent task force" which exists in most organizations for the purpose of taking care of random assignments, i.e., those tasks which need attention but do not fit within any existing organizational function, and (b) job rotation for managers. With regard to the latter, it is Japanese custom for a manager to work toward becoming a generalist rather than maintain a particular specialty. To facilitate this development, managers rotate from one area of specialization to another. Moreover, if a person wants to progress to the ranks of top management, he must work for several years in, say, personnel, even though his original training may have been engineering. It is an exception for the chief executive of a U.S. company to have previously been the head of corporate personnel and prior to that a plant manager.

Tolerance for ambiguity may cause frustration among Americans who usually are more straightforward and assertive, and more prone to conflict.

But the Japanese, who have been conditioned to work together in congested circumstances for more than four centuries, are accustomed to be more sensitive to the needs of others in the same organization. The whole system is developed to cater to be better at mind-reading in the vague, twilight and grey zones. Furthermore, under the influence of perhaps Zen Buddhism, the Japanese intrinsically have a deep-rooted suspicion of what is clearly defined or stated. We believe the truth is in the grey zone. For instance, if you say "my marriage is simply wonderful," we suspect you are not telling the truth. However, if you say "my marriage is an entire mistake," we also doubt its validity. But when you say "my marriage is a wonderful mistake," we feel now you are talking and telling us the truth.

Tolerance of ambiguity also has one more advantage. In a rapidly changing situation, if you define everything — functions, tasks, duties, you will undoubtedly fall into inefficient operations, rigid disfunction, red tape, slowdown of work, and poorer performance, as I experienced in the St. Moritz Hotel last Friday morning. A maitre d' only allocates the seats and does nothing else. A busboy only cleans the table and does nothing else. A waitress serves the guests and does nothing else. It took one hour and a half before we finished a simple continental breakfast that morning. This doesn't usually happen in Japan. Accustomed to work in undifferentiated positions without job specifications, a group of Japanese workers usually trained to be multi-skilled and committed to support each other, could handle the similar situation far more effectively and satisfactorily.

The ingredients for better teamwork we learned from your behavioral scientist are:

1. Sharing the group objective.
2. Sharing the group involvement and commitment.

3. Sharing the decision-making process (though the consensual decision-making may take more time, but requires less time in implementing the plan once decided).
4. Sharing the information (that's why almost all Japanese companies have many meetings).
5. Sharing mutually supporting behavior.

One final point:

The Japanese reluctance to lay off or dismiss people, unless they are really forced to do so as a last resort, stems also from the concept of the organization not simply as a mechanical but an organic unit.

Therefore, when something is wrong with your finger (part of your organization), they aren't as likely to chop off your finger as a surgeon; they'll encourage you to drink herb medicine or administer acupuncture, or give a long tender message to stimulate and heal the ailing limb.

This wholistic and integrated approach to view and act in the organization as a totally functioning, organic system is one of the most fundamental assumptions the Japanese share. I do hope these illustrations may contribute to clarifying some of the basic assumptions underlying Japanese organizational behavior, which is being challenged today through exposure to the entirely new American value system and environment.

Japan:
Its Changing Life Style and Patterns

I. **INTRODUCTION**

While I was listening attentively to my respected colleagues on this panel, I could not help recalling one of the stories I learned when I was studying here some twenty years ago on a Fulbright scholarship (thanks to your American taxpayers) — about an industrial efficiency expert. (Incidentally, some of the audience may have wondered what Sangyo Noritsu College, which appears in the program as my institution, means in Japanese. It literally means "industrial efficiency" and its official translation is Institute of Business Administration and Management.)

In an effort to identify the problem faced by a company, this efficiency expert asked a supervisor of a plant, "What's your problem?" The answer was "lack of communication." Then he went to another shop and asked the same question. The reply was exactly the same — lack of communication. Then he asked one other supervisor of the same company and got the same answer.

So this efficiency expert wrote in his organizational diagnosis report to the top management that the fundamental trouble with this organization is OVERLAPPING.

Having said that I must hasten to add that I do not intend to be critical of my colleagues. I simply want to suggest that my following presentation may be more or less identical with the previous speakers', even though I try to take a somewhat different approach, emphasizing changing work ethics and value systems in organizational life.

Since an expert by definition is a man who creates complexity and confusion out of simplicity, please bear with me for a few minutes.

But in the interest of time, I would like to limit my initial discussion to only two areas — namely the impact of the aging population in Japan and the question of affluence.

II. AGING POPULATION AND ITS IMPACT ON SOCIAL LIFE

Seriously, one of the major concerns to most of us Japanese is the sudden discovery and realization of the rapid aging of our population.

Improved public health and sanitation, which started with DDT spray by G.I. in occupied Japan right after the end of the war, better nutrition than ever before (even though we eat, as compared to American consumers, only 1/20 the beef, 1/3 the dairy products and 1/2 the sugar), more physical exercise (you can find hundreds of Japanese people jogging around the Imperial Palace though they never bothered to buy and read Mr. Fixx's *Complete Book of Running*), dissemination of high-quality child care knowledge triggered by Dr. Spock's book—all these and other factors have definitely contributed to raise our longevity above yours.

We realized that we have the tremendous task of accommodating a greater number of aging people within the time span of only 45 years, while it took from 75—170 years in most Western countries to get adjusted to these demographic changes.

Please imagine for a moment that until the end of World War II, our average life expectancy was somewhere under 50 years for half a century. Now the average life expectancies are 73 for males and 78 for females.

The United Nations classifies countries with less than 4 percent of the population 65 years or over as "young countries," and countries with more than seven percent in this age bracket as "old countries." Japan became an "old country," according to this definition, in 1970.

This quiet and invisible revolution did not stir or alarm the Japanese public, in general, as keenly as the "Nixon Shokku," "Oil Embargo Shokku," or the recent "Iran Shokku." Until recently, Japan unfortunately was not at all ready both socially and institutionally to meet with these new changes. But unless Japan faces this new challenge squarely and takes a positive attitude to overcome the various difficulties caused by the changes, this will give a fatal blow to our future politically, economically and socially. And I think we have a lot to learn from USA, our mentor in this regard.

In order to illustrate the point, let me describe to you one episode which I personally found quite shocking to observe. This sad example concerns the ever-increasing visits by old people (mostly women) to a temple in Nara, commonly known as "Pokkuri Temple." *Pokkuri* means a sudden peaceful death without distress. It is such a tragic and shameful scene to watch hundreds of elderly people seriously praying to Buddha for a peaceful sudden death without suffering from any protracted illness, by placing a pair of undergarments on the altar, which symbolizes the desire of aged people not to undergo any humiliating experience.

Observing this, I was reminded of a piece of news I read in The New York Times during my exchange student days in the late '50s. It was the diary of an old lady who died unnoticed and went undiscovered for almost 2 weeks. She wrote, "No visitor, today. Today nobody called. No friend visited today . . . " As a young student, brought up in a closely-knit family atmosphere, I could not help but feel "Oh, what a dark age of social security in the midst of affluence!" But now this is our immediate problem.

Of course, there have been accelerated efforts to cope with these new situations in all aspects of social life before it gets too late. For instance, the Japanese government has strongly urged all employers to extend the compulsory retirement age of 55 to 60 or more. (According to a survey by Ministry of Labor, 40 percent of companies still set the mandatory retirement age at 55, but 20 percent between 56-59, and 40 percent have extended to 60 years.)

Fortunately, 8 percent of aged people live with their children (which is much higher than USA). Our savings ratio is one of the highest in the world. (This is another example of our concern for rainy days.)

It was only last week that the advisory council on social security recommended the government to raise the coverage of the national pension scheme and expand the number of targeted recipients.

The last example will be a so-called "Silver (for grey haired people) Seminar" especially devised by Mitsubishi Electric Enterprise Union. The program, which is designed to help reassess realistically the middle- and old-aged union members' lives as well as intra-company goals, cope with middle-age stress, refine and redefine their priorities, and diversify their emotional portfolio. It may sound somewhat sinister that the very first session of the seminar is solely devoted to forcing participants to write wills to their beloved wives.

Nevertheless, since our postwar cultures have been primarily youth-oriented or youth-obsessed until 10 years ago when we had large-scale student riots and rebellions, it is still middle-aged and old-aged people who are sacrificed to achieve these gear shifts in forming a new social system.

Therefore, you can see or hear for some time to come innumerable stories related to this painful social readjustment.

For instance, 80 percent of the currently unemployed people are in the age bracket of 44-64 in Japan, whereas it is far less in the USA.

Another good recent example to illustrate this point is the much publicized cruel treatment to *madogiwa-zoku* people. *Madogiwa,* literally means window-side and *zoku,* species of people. They are the middle- and/or old-aged workers, figuratively speaking, on the brink of the company windows to be readily kicked out or bumped out, because employers consider them to have become incompetent and nonpromotable in the company organization.

III. ARE WE REALLY AFFLUENT?

Now I think I have spent too much time on the question of the aging population and its impact on society. Therefore, I would like to call your attention to the second concern or bewilderment shared by most Japanese nowadays. This is the question of our "affluence." Despite the fact we do not feel at all affluent or rich, we found ourselves, to our great surprise, in a very awkward position with everybody in the world repeatedly calling us "Japan the Super Economic Power" and telling us we enjoy the highest GNP per capita in free countries, second only to the United States, and that we are supposed to be filthy rich people.

This perception gap is very real (at least) to us. Yes, as some of the major economic indices show us clearly, statistically speaking we look "rich."

For instance, our per capita income in 1978 might have reached almost the same level as U.S. — much earlier than the prophecy of futurist guru H. Kahn — because of the appreciation of the yen of almost 20 percent in a year. However, this has to be considerably discounted on the basis of actual purchasing power when compared, and it is generally assumed that our real income level is approximately equal to (between) 1/2 — 2/3 of your standard.

Almost every Japanese household is now equipped with all kinds of electric appliances such as TVs, tape-recorders, refrigerators—you name it and we have it—and with subcompact cars and Hondas.

With a population growth rate of only 1 percent, we are now fortunately free from a population explosion, unlike our South-East Asian friends.

Last year 3.5 million people traveled abroad, and bought up all sorts of luxury items and exquisite products like Gucci or Louis Vuitton in Paris, and ate at 200 Japanese restaurants now existing in New York City.

There is no escape from these facts. But we actually can't believe we are affluent. Why do we feel differently? One reason is the magic of currency exchange rates.

An average Japanese worker annually earns about 2.3 million yen, including the semi-annual bonuses which usually equal in total 4 months pay. It is equivalent to $11,000.00 with a 220-yen-to-a-dollar ratio, but a little less than $10,000.00 computed with a 240-yen-rate at the end of 1977, and $6,500.00 when a new floating system started in the Smithsonian Institution back in 1971.

Recently a confidential report of the European Community was disclosed where the E.C. labels Japan "a nation of workaholics who live in what Westerners would regard as little more than rabbit hutches." Undoubtedly, many Japanese were infuriated by this racist undertone. But I could sympathize with their frustration which apparently stems from our nearly $7 billion trade surplus with the E.C. (I should not need to remind you here in this connection that our trade surplus with you was much greater in 1978 at $12 billion.)

But, more basically, what I would like to stress here is that the E.C.'s harsh and cynical commentary is quite valid and our so-called affluence is nothing but a skin-deep, superficial, fragile prosperity.

Let us go a step further with you in a "quality of life" list to explore our actual living environment.

There you can see:
1) We still have comparatively poorly paved roads.
2) Our sewage systems are still underdeveloped (though modernized vacuum honey-bucket cars are antiquated.)
3) Homes and apartment rooms are small (almost half or 1/3 of your size and slightly better than rabbit hutches.)
4) Public parks are below standard.
5) There are public bath houses in large cities designed for underprivileged people living in bath-less rooms (though now they are divided for the sexes.)

Therefore as far as amenities of life and really substantial progress are concerned, we are still far behind the general level of civilized Western countries.

It is in this area that Japan must work very hard (correction — very effectively — no more workaholic image) to build a pleasant living environment and guarantee a stable livelihood through the establishment of a decent, meaningful social security system, provision of sufficient and adequate housing, promotion of environmental protection policies and spending of ample "social capital or overhead."

IV. CHANGING WORK ETHICS?

Now let me move on to the third problem area I want to discuss and share with you this evening — namely the changing work ethics or basic orientation of people.

Now let's briefly review the situations. You will undoubtedly find it interesting to note the different attitudes toward life between Americans and Japanese when asked, in a forced-choice type questionnaire, about the basic preference of life style. More than 75 percent of Americans replied they preferred an unrestricted, free-wheeling life pattern, while about half the Japanese agreed with this idea.

But while only 6.2 percent of Americans wanted economic affluence, 35.4 percent of Japanese (six times greater) still aspire to achieve affluence. (This may prove the point I raised a few minutes ago about the lack of sufficient social amenities.)

You will find another interesting difference in attitudes toward job satisfaction. Whereas 70.7 percent of Americans responded that they find satisfaction beyond their work, only 48.5 percent of our workaholic Japanese answered that what they find worthwhile is other than work. (But a footnote here is necessary. There is a tendency on the part of Americans to differentiate job satisfaction from other satisfaction. What I want to clarify here is that Japanese management has traditionally encouraged the company trip or holiday, company-sponsored baseball matches, and company sponsored 'go' tournaments as measures to boost employee loyalty and sense of belonging.)

What I want to stress here is that as the years go by, the Japanese in general are becoming more and more inclined toward leisure than toward work-related activity.

Now let us take a closer look at what the Japanese seek for satisfaction in their work places. That complex graph indicates a number of significant differences.

1) For example, you will see the currently underprivileged and frustrated female workers noticeably want to have more responsibility in work.
2) Older people, quite naturally, want responsibility worthy of their age and seek better interpersonal relations.

About ten years ago, I made a survey of almost 100 female office workers and junior secretaries working in downtown Tokyo to identify their reactions to unhappiness or frustration on the job.

No. 1   Talk it out with a friend to let off steam.
No. 2   Shop and spend impulsively.
No. 3   Drink sake.
No. 4   Cut hair short or change hair style.

It is also interesting to note that there exists the cultural difference in handling job dissatisfaction. You can clearly see that patient and obedient acceptance of the situation is definitely higher among Japanese. This may result partly from the influence and partly from lifetime employment and seniority-directed practices. Americans are obviously more inclined toward Avis-Rent-a-Car's philosophy of "trying harder."

Even though we are plagued with very keen competition to

get into the prestigious higher educational institutions to obtain passports for greater status and income as was already described by Prof. Iwao, it is quite interesting to note that only 14.1 percent of Japanese young people think the academic record counts as the important ingredient for success in life.

If you combine senior high graduates in Upper-Middle and Lower-Middle class categories (which becomes 80.3 percent), and compare this figure to another combination of figures of people with higher education in the same categories $(57.7 + 26.4 = 84.1)$, you will find no significant difference between these two social classes.

This might indicate that the Japanese business organization is still "porous" enough vertically and less rigidly stratified to permit people with less education to climb the organizational ladder of success if they are competent enough and determined to get ahead.

One final comment about the chart on job change. Another difference is manifest here. Horizontal mobility among Japanese young people, though gradually changing, is still limited as compared to your people.

V. CONCLUSION

Let me briefly sum up what I want to convey to you this evening.

1) Japanese society is rapidly getting older, thus youth-oriented culture and values will have to undergo drastic changes socially, institutionally and organizationally.
2) So-called Japanese "affluence" is not to be confused with your affluence. Japan has to pay for its past economic success and make up for the heretofore neglected social amenities.
3) Our "work hard ethic," with higher levels of education

and technical skills which played a crucial role in generating remarkable postwar economic growth, may have to go through gradual changes, but not to the degree of entire erosion.

The Japanese are now in the process of re-orienting themselves and seeking a new identity for the 1980s.

However, as a charter member of the "cautious optimist club" I do believe Japan is able to solve all these problems, if she can be fully aware of her own strength and build up solutions on these strengths. One conspicuous strength is adaptability. Because we are flexible in our social and value system, we find it much easier to change. Our typical way of solving major social problems for the past 2,000 years has been successful application of this group problem-solving process.

II

How to Do Business in Japan (1)
Joy and Agony of Learning Japanese

Last week, a young American businessman, who is a self-styled, top-notch playboy, complained to me how deceptive the Japanese language was. He said that he had seen a neon sign over a Ginza night spot that assured him he would have a chance to meet and get acquainted with a charming Japanese girl. But after drinking quite a few drinks served elegantly by the lovely hostesses roving in musical chair fashion, he failed to make any headway in finding a partner for the night. He was so furious at the deception in the name of the bar which enticed him and made him believe in the certainty of scoring for the night.

I asked half-irritatedly, "What the hell was the name of that bar?" I could file a case with the Japanese Better Business Bureau for tricking this poor tourist. He answered, "The name is SURE-SURE." The moment I heard him pronounce the bar's name 'SHUR SHUR,' I could not help bursting into laughter, because SURE-SURE as pronounced *"sooray-sooray"* in

Japanese is not 'sure, sure' and does not mean certain, but 'close to or nearly illegal' or 'being on bad terms.'

A recent report on Japan indicates that one out of ten Japanese can manage somehow to communicate with people from abroad in English about simple day-to-day matters.

On the other hand, a growing number of people abroad have apparently started to learn the Japanese language as the economic position of Japan in the world market rises. I was surprised to find recently that in an IBM plant located in Raleigh, North Carolina, some twenty computer engineers were intensively studying Japanese three times a week for three months on company time. In Baltimore, I was greatly amazed to meet a young, intelligent assistant professor of Japanese politics, teaching at Johns Hopkins University. She was a graduate of Harvard and Princeton and she knew all the details of all conflicts between Rono-ha (Labor and farmer collaboration school) and Koza-ha (Ivory tower faculty school) of the 1920's Japanese Marxist theorists. She shocked me even more because she was not only an expert on prewar development of the Marxist movement in Japan, but because she demonstrated her wider and deeper understanding of Japanese society and history at large.

Almost every month, when I serve regularly as a host to an early morning business-oriented radio program called "World Hotline 1134 JOQR," broadcast on Wednesday and Thursday, I have the pleasure of chatting over the international telephone with an English businessman based in London, owner of a trading company.

I have never met him personally, but he speaks very refined good Japanese with no accent, which actually led some of the listeners to believe he was Japanese.

As these examples vividly tell us, the number of people in the world actively pursuing the study of Japanese has evidently increased recently, although there are differences in their levels of proficiency.

Despite the fact I personally experienced tremendous difficulty in familiarizing myself with English, I forgot how complex and tiring learning Japanese must be for foreigners until I met an exchange student from Nigeria. He challenged me by saying, "Kobayashi-san, what do you say in Japanese when you have one pen?" Of course, "*Pen ippon.*" He asked me, "How about two pens?" My answer was naturally, "*Pen ni-hon.*" Then triumphantly he asked me, "What about three pens?" I replied, "*Pen sanbon.*" In responding to his successive questions, I realized that the Japanese numerical suffixes used in counting are quite confusing to beginners, even though we take it for granted and are not bothered at all, because of the natural learning process during childhood.

According to a study by U.S. State Department language specialists, Japanese is ranked as LEVEL 4 together with Chinese, Korean and Arabic. The LEVEL 4 difficulty language requires the average student to spend at least 1,200 intensive learning hours to become "reasonably fluent." As contrasted to these hard-to-master languages, LEVEL 1 languages such as Dutch and Indonesian only demand 340 hours.

But if this leads you to believe that Japanese is impossible for people from overseas, you are mistaken, and if you don't try, you will miss the joy and beauty and convenience of conversing in Japanese.

As readers are probably well aware the Japanese language is composed of three main types of written characters: *kanji, hiragana,* and *katakana.* Roman letters and Arabic numerals are also sometimes mixed with the other three types, but not frequently.

Kanji characters are ideograms which were introduced to

Japan from China about 1,800 years ago, and the Chinese and Japanese readings of them, today's two types of Japanese alphabets — *hiragana* and *katakana* — were devised. At present we use about three thousand kanji characters including 1,850 "daily-use characters."

Since *kanji* is originally based upon pictures, it is fun to use one's imagination to decipher their meanings. If you know a simple character like *tree*, you can readily understand that two trees standing together (as an ideogram) means — *wood*. When you see another tree standing on top of these two tree characters, yes, you guess right — it means *deep forest*. If you learn a *kanji* which signifies a woman, what do you think three women grouped together in a *kanji* ideogram means? — Gossipy? Close enough. Noisy? Better still. It usually signifies *noisy*.

Another reason your study of Japanese will be exciting and facile is the abundance of imported words from abroad, particularly from Europe and America. One dictionary of imported Japanese lists 16,000 commonly used Japanese words imported from abroad. They are especially numerous in business. Therefore if you pronounce each word carefully and distinctly but with less accentuation, you can communicate with your Japanese colleagues by speaking mostly borrowed words for example, "Yuni-Bakku-No-Nyu-Kompyuta-Sisutemuwa-Ekuserento-de-mentenansumo-iizii-dashi-paafoumansumo-appugureido-dekiru." (A new computer system of Univac is excellent and its maintenance is easy and performance can be upgraded.)

Among the deluge of imported Japanese words, *Up* and *High* (or *Hi*) are most frequently used and misused favorites. Hi-Lotion Shampoo, Toyota Hiace, High-Stainless cutting knife and Hi-Eclair candy, Hi-Nikka whisky and Hi-milk chocolate, High sense suit, and Hi roast instant coffee are typical examples of Japanese brand names.

Another favorite and abused word borrowed from English is *UP*. Wage increase is *beisu-UP* (base-up); improving one's image is *imeiji-UP* (image-up); better living, *raife UP* (life-up); energizing, *pawaa-UP* (power up); and becoming more charming, *chaamu UP* (charm up).

So why not try to pick up a few Japanese words and try them out on your business friends for ice-breaking or building better rapport. *Endo-desu*. (The End — that's all for today.)

How to Do Business in Japan (2)
Study Denies 'Closed Japan' Concept; Shows Opportunities for Success

To most businessmen and politicians from overseas and even some Japanese, the mere mention of the Japanese market usually suggests "a huge, perhaps rich, but entirely closed garden." The generally shared view among those people about the Japanese market is that it is heavily guarded by visible and invisible trade barriers and protected by the all-powerful MITI (Ministry of International Trade and Industry) in close collaboration with another equally influential institution, Keidanren (Federation of Economic Organizations). Therefore no foreign enterprises are able to penetrate successfully this lucrative arena despite immense effort and sophisticated modern marketing techniques.

This commonly-held notion was proved to be nothing but an utter fiction in a recent joint U.S. and Japan study. Despite the more or less extensive circulation last year of the report which denounced the prevailing misconception of a "tightly controlled Japanese market," this important document seemingly was not generally well received by those who are concerned with entering this market. One may suspect that the naked truth about the easy accessibility of the Japanese market is uncomfortable news to some, for it exposes the lack of sufficient effort by those who attempt to participate in the market. The report, entitled "JAPAN: Obstacles and Opportunities," was prepared by McKinsey & Company, Inc. for the United States-Japan Study Group.

One of the most revealing results made available by this conscientious study is that the total export volume of the United States to Japan is greater than generally perceived and the penetration of U.S. exports into the Japanese market is also greater than popularly acknowledged. Although U.S. imports account for little less than 2 percent, this figure is almost 50 percent greater than Japan's penetration (1.3 percent) of the United States. With this remarkable expose, the book also indicates that Japan, "though a difficult and fiercely competitive market, is far less controlled than commonly believed and in fact, is no more closed or controlled from the legal standpoint than some Western markets."

The study's conclusion is: "Viewing quotas in perspective, Japan restricts just 27 product categories of which only five are non-agricultural items. This compares favorably with other countries' non-agricultural quota categories (e.g., United States' six, West Germany's 11, and France's 27 non-agricultural items). In terms of overall tariffs, Japan's average of 3.2 percent, which includes recent reductions, is below most developed nations including the United States and European countries."

The study further discloses four important areas where winners in the Japanese market are highly visible: a resource-driven product; technological lead; a "new-to-Japan" concept; or a differentiated marketing strategy to aim at a special niche in the market. Typical examples of successes using the first resource-driven products are the oil companies. Mobil, Esso, Shell and Caltex are all household names to the Japanese people.

A second area in which overseas firms enjoy comfortable market positions are plastic engineering, liquid crystals, mainframe computers, copying machines, Teflon, and other pharmaceuticals. For example, we cook our barbeque and prepare crepes or Japanese-style pancake called *okonomiyaki* on a Teflon-coated electric pan. Our forty thousand drycleaners use Teflon-coated shirt pressing machines every day in all prefectures of Japan. Contac, Bufferin, and Band Aids are found in most Japanese families' first aid boxes.

The third product and service entry area, namely "new to Japan," offers abundant winning examples. Instant coffee, be it Nestle, or Maxwell, once unknown to Japanese consumers is now a daily necessity.

Safety razors, such as Schick, Braun and Gillete, completely eliminated the traditional *kamisori* (traditional razors). Fast food chains like McDonalds, unknown to Japanese families only a short time ago, now take pride in being the most profitable and productive operation of all the McDonalds sections.

The fourth area, which the report terms "special niche" again provides us with ample evidence that far-sighted entrepreneurs have caught the pulse of the changing Japanese consumer market. For instance, brand-name luggage such as Louis Viton is not confined to top income bracket people in Japan but is actually carried even by office ladies newly recruited from senior high school.

Moreover, this TSG (Trade Study Group) report identified three major factors, common to all the successful entrants to the Japanese market. Success factor No. 1 in their analysis is *com-*

mitment. The report frankly tells us that the U.S. firms with long term success in Japan have made a significant commitment in time, money and effort and have solved the delicate human relations problems that naturally arise from cross-cultural differences.

Success factor No. 2 according to the report is *creativity*. Here creativity means flexible adjustment to local tastes and strategic maneuvering to adapt to the local preferences. The report quotes Wella's case as a familiar example of a creative approach to the Japanese market instead of competing head-on with Japanese manufacturers.

The last C for success factor in Japan is *competitiveness*. Dr. Michael Porter of the Harvard Business School, the authoritative business strategist who has been nick-named the 'Sun Tzu' of the modern business world by some Japanese, confided to me his thoughts on the Japanese market. When he had his first public seminar on corporate strategy at the Hotel Okura in April 1983 attended by more than 400 businessmen, he said, "If you can survive in this very fierce Japanese market, you can be a winner in any part of the world."

Furthermore, the report was able to uncover the four fundamental traits of the winners in Japan. First, they are able to tailor their products to the demands, tastes and very particular requirements of Japanese consumers as Playboy products did in appealing to Japanese consumers' egos. Second, most of them have cautiously selected Japanese counterparts to complement their original strength. Diner's Club worked with Japan Travel Bureau as their partner, and Phizer appointed Taito as their collaborator. Third as we pointed out earlier, all of them have made heavy up-front investment and revised product lines and specifications to meet specific local demands. Fourth, they have delegated authority to local management very effectively. Xerox is now under the leadership of Mr. Yotaro Kobayashi who originally came from Fuji Photo film. Seven-Eleven Japan is making impressive strides in attracting 800,000 customers every day through the excellent leadership of Ito-Yokado's Toshifumi Suzuki.

After examining the report, I could not help recalling a story which seems to be quite applicable to the present situation of the foreign businessman in Japan. It is a story about two salesmen from Europe who visited a less developed country some time ago. One of the salesmen sent a cable back home "PLS FORWARD FIVE MILLION SHOES BECAUSE NOBODY WEARS ANY SHOES," whereas the other salesman sent a telegram to his office, saying "IMPOSSIBLE TO SELL ANY SHOES BECAUSE NOBODY WEARS SHOES HERE."

How to Do Business in Japan (3)
A Key to Doing Business with the Japanese: Tolerance for Ambiguity

One of the most frustrating experiences which is widely shared by foreign businessmen is the ambiguous and nebulous reaction of their Japanese counterparts. Those Western or Western-oriented business people who seek quick and clear-cut responses almost constantly time suffer from roundabout and vague replies.

One shrewd student of cross-cultural communication at International Christian University once wrote a prize-winning thesis entitled "19 Ways of Saying 'No' Without Actually saying 'No'." Therefore, if a reply runs, "I will let my boys check it," or "That is very difficult" or "We have no budget" the innocent foreigners are usually advised not to expect any positive answers from the persons with whom they are negotiating. The one they should be most careful of is, "I will do it with a forward-looking attitude." The poor American negotiators who received these "words of assurance" from the late Prime

Minister Eisaku Sato had to wait some time before they realized this literal translation of "Maemukino shisei de zensho shimasu" is frequently a synonym of the very polite Japanese "No."

The reasons for the alleged ambiguity and misleadingly unclear replies are numerous. The first and foremost cause often mentioned by Japanologists is the fact that the Japanese can comfortably and unmistakably communicate with each other because of their homogeneity. The Japanese have lived for many centuries as a homogeneous people or an isolated archipelago—perhaps this has minimized the necessity for articulate communication among them. This kind of built-in rapport is evident when one meets a typical old Japanese couple and find out the only words the husband needs after returning from the day's work are *yu* (bath) and *meshi* (meal).

The second favorite cliche-like analysis of this syndrome is the face-saving behavior among Orientals, particularly Japanese. In order to live harmoniously in a densely populated community like Japan with traditional hierarchies in organizations, one must be extremely cautious not to hurt the feelings of others by calling a spade a spade. The use of the honorific styles of Japanese language further augments the complications in the conventional networks of mutual communication.

Third, the basic concept of Zen Buddhism might have exerted its influence on the seemingly confusing Japanese communication behaviors. Zen philosophy, which attempts to eliminate all media, written or spoken, as deterrents and barriers for grasping the reality of man and nature, blatantly distrusts and doubts the functions of the language and words. Therefore, Zen Buddhists throw apparently silly and contradictory questions in the form of *Ko-an* (catechetic question or riddle) to challenge the Aristotelian two-valued approach and Western type of excessive dependence on language for real communication or communion with the real self.

This kind of cultural diagnosis suggests that the Japanese are conditioned historically to be more comfortable when they face ambiguous situations and expressions, and feel less frustrated than those people who have been accustomed to think in terms of a black and white approach. The Japanese are used to viewing the spectrum or continuum as a wholistic entity. Suppose we ask a non-Japanese couple who have been married, say, more than twenty years, "How is your marriage?" If the answer to this question is "Our marriage is simply wonderful," we doubt that they are giving the whole truth. We suspect that during the past two decades of marriage there have been at least some ups and downs, and think that marriage cannot be described in such simplistic terms.

If on the other hand the reply to that question is a "Oh, our marriage is dire mistake and failure," although the couple is not divorced, we also think this is not the whole truth and reality of the marriage. However, if the answer is "Our marriage is a wonderful mistake!" we are fully convinced that they are telling the whole truth and disclosing the true secret of their married life. The last question, which ordinary Japanese could easily sympathize with, may sound self-contradictory to Western minds. But to most Japanese who tend to think that truth does not lie in two extremes, this kind of seemingly illogical response could be widely accepted as an authentic reflection of reality in life.

Dr. Harlon Cleaveland, former dean of the University of Hawaii, in his lucidly written book *The Future Executive* endorsed this type of 'Japaneasy' acceptance or higher degree of tolerance of ambiguity, when he said "success in managing a web of tensions requires a taste for ambiguity." He further points out "the many-sidedness of real executive problems suggests a made-up word: 'ambi-' means two-sided, so it might better be called a taste for polyguity.) If the inside of each organization can be described as a web of tensions, its outside relations — with clients, veto groups, bank, union, special-interest associations, public agencies and legislatures—can be seen a larger tension system, with executives at each switching station trying to bring people together with a view to taking a next step. The prizes go to those who can move toward their subjective human purposes by tolerating a high degree of polyguity in return for a maximum amount of action." The recent works of behavioral scientists and organization development practitioners join in underlining the importance of being less disturbed under the complex and volatile circumstances where a multitude of new developments and unknown variables confuse and dominate business assessment and decision-making.

A number of surveys which are designed to identify the 'pet' mottos and favorite quotations of Japanese C.E.Os (Chief Executive Officers) in business and industry indicate that the most frequently quoted ones are inconsistent and paradoxical on the surface. For instance, the top-ranked saying loved by a great number of Japanese business leaders is *shoshin ni shite daitan* which literally means "Cowardly cautious, but at the same time courageously audacious." Another example to the same effect is a quotation from a Chinese strategist, Sun Tzu (B.C. 515-496) in the *Art of War:* "In peace prepare for war; in war prepare for peace." Shingen Takeda (1521-1573), one of the powerful Japanese war lords during the Great Civil War Age used to carry his war banner in which he used abridged symbols for his war tactics, derived from the same Sun Tzu's book of strategy: *fu* (wind), *rin* (wood), *ka* (fire) and *zan* (mountain). "Fu-Rin-Ka-Zan" originates from Sun Tzu's discourse and means that the effective leaders behave quick as wind, quiet as wood, aggressive as fire and stable as a mountain. In April 1983, I had a chance to attend the wedding reception of the heir apparent of one of the biggest toy manufacturing tycoons in Tokyo. Mr. Michio Watanabe, the former minister of finance, told the story of his chat with British Prime Minister Thatcher. When he was asked by the lady prime minister during the last summit conference about his motto of preference, Mr. Watanabe quoted from one of the oldest Buddhist sutra, "Ku soku ze shiki and shiki soku ze ku (Void is like full, full is like void)." We missed the probably bewildered reaction of the prime minister to this mystifying Oriental answer. But to approximately 1,000 participants of this huge social function, the message of the motto appeared easily comprehended.

One of the current non-fiction best sellers in the U.S.A. market is *In Search of Excellence — Lessons from America's Best-Run Companies* by Thomas J. Peters and Robert H. Waterman Jr. After studying carefully forty-two high performing corporations for the past twenty years, the authors could identify eight attributes that emerged to characterize most clearly the distinction of excellent, innovative American companies. One key parameter distinguishing effective companies is simultaneous loose-tight properties. Thus, the authors emphasize that excellent companies are both centralized and decentralized at the same time. And these good companies are analyzed as being always on the brink of falling into chaos. In light of this analysis, one may safely conclude that despite all the clamor about cross-cultural differences and perception gaps and value abyss, really high-performance organizations do not know of any national boundaries and share the same or similar attributes wherever they operate. Thus, the so-called Japanese higher degree of tolerance for ambiguity and hazy behavioral patterns may not be unique to the Japanese and may be prevalent among any effectively operated organizations in this modern turbulent world, in the final analysis.

How to Do Business in Japan (4)

Permanent Employment, Seniority Wage System, Enterprise Union Structure — Are All These Simply Myths?

In discussing the unique characteristics of Japanese business organizations, the most popular and frequently quoted models are the three interlocking institutions of permanent employment, a seniority wage system, and an enterprise union structure. Unfortunately, one of the most common and most disheartening aspects of behavior and the thinking process is that once a belief or perception takes root, it often exerts a distorting influence on the realistic understanding of the truth. A case in point is the deep-rooted myths surrounding these three subsystems of Japanese organizational activities. The myths are very much the creation of the wishful thinking of Japanese business people who wish to embellish the Japanese business climate.

Let's examine each of these "Three Sacred Treasures of the Structure of Japanese Business."

Whether you call it a permanent, lifelong or lifetime

employment system, the actual recipients of this job security arrangement are confined to only 25 percent of the entire Japanese work force. If you believe all Japanese workers are enjoying the benefits of job security until they reach retirement age, you are completely wrong. Job guarantees of this sort are limited to a mere quarter of the Japanese labor force, particularly those full-time employees in the larger corporations. Temporary, seasonal, and part-time workers are not covered by this much acclaimed humane practice, even though they too may be employed directly by the large and established companies. Moreover, one survey by the Japanese Ministry of Labor clearly shows that about 45 percent of those workers between 20 and 29 years of age change their jobs at least once and some 25 percent of those between 30 and 44 do so also. This survey includes Japanese firms with more than five employees. Another survey of 'Employee Trends' by the same ministry provides more shocking facts for those naive believers in the humane paternalism of Japanese business. The separation rate, that is, voluntary quitting, of workers aged under 19 is a surprising 20 percent. Furthermore, as contrasted to a 44.1 percent turnover in the U.S., the turnover rate in the same age bracket for Japan is 57.8 percent.

Therefore, Japanese workers are very mobile and willingly or unwillingly do change jobs very often, particularly among the young, less educated employees hired by small companies. Those Japanese businessmen who criticize the 80 percent annual labor turnover of the American workers in California or the 100 percent job-hopping rate among Singaporian sales clerks, and praise the established Japanese permanent employment system are thus taking refuge in an unrealistic myth.

More Emphasis on Performance

The firm believers in the seniority wage structure will also find themselves standing on less than solid ground. Recent statistics point out that the value of seniority in determining Japanese wages has dramatically dwindled and now constitutes less than 60 percent of the assessment on the national average. In the case of workers 50 and over, seniority accounts for only approximately 34 percent of their entire salary.

Furthermore, the traditional "seniority-based determinants" are composed of age, length of service, education, and sometimes experience. These factors, usually referred to as seniority or personal factors, play a dominant role in setting the wages or salaries for those freshly recruited from colleges and senior-high schools for the first 10 years of their career with a company.

But, after a decade of more or less stable annual increases, new criteria are introduced by larger firms, which make sharp discriminations among the employees with respect to wages on the basis of merit. The research by Dr. Mitsuyo Hanada furnishes us with a revealing pattern of three distinct salary increase curves and career paths in major Japanese corporations which begin to take their distinctive paths after about 10 years of service with the corporation in the case of college graduates. Top management candidates or those with similar potential, of course, enjoy a sharp upturn in their earnings. Middle-management-caliber colleagues are placed in jobs which provide a somewhat less dramatic increase in annual earnings, whereas the lowest rated personnel are entitled to only a minimal guaranteed annual increase for the rest of their business lives.

To illustrate the point, I can cite the specific example of two simultaneously recruited university graduates at a major Japanese bank. After serving 20 years at the bank, one fellow earns close to 12 million yen per year, while his classmate makes only 6.5 million yen.

Various studies indicate that in most Japanese large and medium-sized firms, wages and salaries in recent years have increasingly been decided more on the basis of merit and performance. One of the latest surveys demonstrates that performance, job classfication function, skill expertise and other job-related factors count more in deciding wage policies and administration than seniority. The report suggests that these criteria together have a weight of nearly 50 percent in setting the wage levels of middle-aged job holders.

Not Killing the Goose

The third myth regarding Japanese management practices is in the domain of its union structure and labor-management relations. Both in Japan and abroad, people tend to characterize Japanese labor-management relations as amicable, harmonious, and collaborative. This kind of description is only a half-truth. Comparing Japanese labor relations with Western counterparts, we are often apt to regard the Japanese unions as docile, company-dominated organizations. In fact this is only half the picture.

Even though the Japanese labor unions are structurally based in a particular corporation, their activities bear little resemblance to the company unions, independent unions or in-house unions so notorious in Western labor history.

With the exception of the Japanese Seamen's Union, all Japanese unions are organized on an enterprise basis. These enterprise unions, even though they form many loose federations or confederations both industrially and nationally, are powerful organizations, each with ample financial and human resources.

Yes, they do collaborate with employers in increasing company profits and productivity. And, of course, they take more care not to kill the goose that lays the golden eggs. But once they go to the negotiation table for collective bargaining, they do fight and exert all their powers in many effective ways, including strikes, to get their share of increased earnings. So labelling the Japanese unions non-adversarial compared to their Western counterparts is incorrect.

The foregoing discussion, I hope, may have dispelled some of the mist generated by the commonly shared myths and stereotypes about Japanese organizational practices. We have a saying, "Confucian scholars are liable to be out of date." In this context the interim report by the Japanese Overseas Enterprise Association published recently makes a decisive contribution to setting straight false assumptions about Japanese management, and their final report to come out next year will undoubtedly do much to lead us from the jungle of misunderstanding about Japanese corporate systems.

How to Do Business in Japan (5)
In Search of Excellent Japanese Companies

In the United States, the management book *In Search of Excellence* by Thomas J. Peters and Robert H. Waterman Jr., had sold more than 1.5 million copies by the end of March, 1984 and its Japanese translation, *Ekuserento Kampanii,* also has recorded phenomenal sales of close to 400,000 copies. Even though the authoritative Harvard Business Review carried in its November-December issue an extremely thorough critique of the book by a "colleague" consultant named Daniel T. Carroll who doubted the validity of the work, we can not overlook the fact that widespread acceptance of the book is an undeniable social phenomenon.

The work by the two management consultants was a big hit because they could, in the first place, offer consolation to millions of American businessmen who were on the brink of losing their self-confidence, battered primarily by seemingly successful Japanese managerial effort.

The book was highly acclaimed because it has tried to restore the pride and prestige of American management by demonstrating evidence of 36 companies that could maintain 20 years' growth and profitability. Thus, our American friends can comfortably say, "We ain't as bad and dumb as some of the management egg-heads assert."

The second reason why the excellence syndrome triggered by the work spreads so quickly and widely is its appeal to common sense. The so-called eight practices universally found in highly-performing companies starting with "bias for action, close to the customers, hand-on value driven, regarding rank and file employees as sources of quality, productivity and profit . . . etc." are not much of a surprise to us. These are all based on a common sense approach rather than magic.

But the irony of their argument is that the knack of putting common sense into action is easier said than done.

Interestingly enough, about eighty Japanese consultants, both inhouse and others who gathered in August 1983 in conference confirmed that the eight principles do apply exactly to the excellent, innovative Japanese companies they have selected, such as Kyocera and Honda, with one exception.

The exception is the seventh role of excellent U.S. corporations which try to keep a "lean staff and slim organizations."

Because of the long-term commitment for job security for employees and primarily seniority-based wage practice, even the good Japanese companies usually have to waver one of the important "management prerogatives" of hire and fire.

Speaking of staying small, the interim report of the study of mini-excellent companies by D. K. Cliford of McKinsey is interesting to note here. Again, all 10 guiding principles and practices observed by high-growing small and medium-sized U.S. businesses also can be applied to their Japanese counterparts

137

with perhaps one exception. Other than motivating with money, the rest of the 10 rules are almost identical with our observations of good, small Japanese firms: regarding innovation as a way of life; creating and developing of small market niches; competing on value, not price; developing strong sense of mission; attending to fundamentals; attacking bureaucratization; encouraging experiments; thinking like customers, and setting examples at the top.

Since most companies, Japanese or American, commit blunders by not implementing common sense in doing business, a few companies that are dedicated and obsessed with quality products and service will stand out as excellent organizations.

As a Japanese saying goes, a few excellent companies become prominent just "as pure, snow-white cranes stand out amidst messy garbage."

According to a study by the Japan Overseas Enterprise Association, one of the ten most frequently asked questions by overseas employees working in Japanese-owned companies abroad is why the Japanese managers and supervisors are so particular about cleaning up the work sites.

This is because they firmly believe that clean workshops are the prerequisite for producing quality products.

There is also the influence of traditional Japanese learning methods. Be it tea ceremony or samurai fencing, novices must endure numberless hours of strict, tiresome, repetitive imitation of model behavior as shown by elders or masters, and an initial stage of cleaning the training environment, before they are actually taught specific skills and techniques.

Now, coming back to excellent Japanese companies, we can point out two more practices in addition to Peters' and Waterman's eighth findings.

If I may borrow a phrase from computer specialists' jargon,

one of the common principles observed by excellent U.S. firms is KISS, "Keep It Simple, Stupid."

But I may add another interpretation of the KISS principle actively operating in growing Japanese companies.

The additional version of KISS is "Keep It Small, Smarty!" When I had an opportunity to interview Mr. Sugiura, chairman of Honda, early this year, I asked him what bothers him most as top manager. He replied, "My greatest concern was and is how we could keep the spirit of a small entrepreneur while at the same time we are growing bigger and bigger."

Thus, Japanese executives are very much aware of the fact that while the word "kiss" can be a noun or verb, it is also an important conjunction for cohesive connection of co-workers in a compact, creative company community.

Therefore, recent applause for WAM or MBWA in the United States is nothing new to Japanese top management. Walking Around Management or Management by Walking Around is a natural and built-in part of, or extension of, their "stay small" orientation.

The second addition to Peters' and Waterman's principles is an encouragement of constant learning and study in dynamically growing Japanese companies.

A classic example would be the case of tremendous savings on long distance telephone bills by the joint effort of QC Circles of telephone operators, both in a Sanwa Bank branch in Osaka and Nippon Steel's office in Nagoya. They learned all seven cost-reduction techniques of QCC, ranging from Pareto charting to fishbone analysis methods.

The *esprit de corps* supported by the "Learn More to Earn More" philosophy is instrumental in advancing and upgrading the performance of Japanese companies. Thus, most of the Japanese excellent companies, long before the authors of *Back-*

to-Basics Management pointed it out, have already practiced the following formulas:

News + Information + Comment = Knowledge

Knowledge + Thinking + Feedback = Understanding

Understanding + Commitment + Discipline = Back-to-Basics Management

The forward-looking Japanese corporations also have tried almost desperately not to abide by "The Rules of Killing Innovation," advocated recently by Dr. Rosabeth M. Kanter in her book, *The Change Masters*. The good firms have cautiously avoided being trapped by "suspicion about ideas, criticism without praise, too tight control, making changes in secret, and pretending tops know everything."

The Japanese change masters did their best not to get caught in the pitfall of becoming "segmentalist companies" so that they would be regarded as "integrative, wide-open team-oriented companies."

How to Do Business in Japan (6)

Ten Questions Most Frequently Asked Japanese Expatriates Working Abroad

As Japanese business expands beyond the borders of the domestic market and penetrates further and deeper into other countries, Japanese companies have suddenly awakened to the reality of their new situation abroad, which far surpasses their traditional and insular-minded way of thinking. Karl Marx's axiom that "quantity alters quality and structure" is extremely self-evident as it relates to Japanese business and its new position towards the world.

As of the end of 1982, Japanese companies operating abroad exceeded ten thousand in number, their accumulated amount of direct investment overseas was presumably more than $5.6 billion and the number of local employees working for these Japan-originated enterprises reached 1.2 million. At the same time, the Japanese Ministry of Foreign Affairs estimates that the total number of Japanese expatriates including their families is now close to 400,000.

This trend to globalization on the part of Japanese multinationals is definitely going to continue. This is primarily because Japanese companies have to go abroad in the form of direct investment to secure and safeguard their existing export market shares in the U.S. and Europe in the face of rising protectionism. The second reason for the accelerated movement of Japanese capital abroad as direct investment is attributable to increasing "resource nationalism." Resource-rich countries are no longer willing to export their raw materials in an unrefined state, but rather want to have them highly processed so that they can earn more foreign currency with these better value-added products. The third reason why Japanese companies are being pushed further into the area of direct investment rather than sticking to their traditional patterns of export and import is the rising cost of the Japanese worker. If we take the average annual earnings before tax of a male in the manufacturing sector with two children and a non-working wife in 1981, Japan ranks second in the world with $18,609. The corresponding figures in the United States and France are $16,471 and $9,815, respectively.

Therefore, Japanese firms that must compete internationally with their increasingly higher wages must either transfer their labor-intensive jobs to less developed countries or automate out and robotize their entire operations to obtain a competitive edge in the world market.

Japanese investment abroad on the whole is still lagging far behind the levels of the other leading advanced nations. At the end of 1981, the U.S. held 47.1 percent of all world private investment abroad, as opposed to 16.5 percent for the U.K., 7.7 percent for West Germany and 5.1 percent for Japan. Thus, Japanese firms must step up their new type of international operations whether they like it or not.

Being a latecomer to the world business scene as an investor and manager, the Japanese must go through the inevitable process of attempting to articulately explain to local businessmen and employees their somewhat different approach to management, especially in the area of human resources and development. In this context, a newly published leaflet entitled "Ten Questions Regarding the Japanese Type of Management" is worthy of note because it is the first attempt on the part of Japanese business circles to respond to the questions most frequently put by local people.

Written in Japanese, English and Chinese (with Thai as a recent addition), the pamphlet illuminates major areas of conflict, doubt and distrust as seen from the standpoint of the local employees of the Japanese multinationals. The booklet puts particular emphasis on the inquiries made most frequently by local lower-ranking personnel in LDCs and NICs.

The very first question taken up by this booklet refers to the so-called "overpresence" of Japanese managers, as follows:

"Why is the number of Japanese in overseas Japanese companies so large? Even in cases where the Japanese staff has been reduced, why is it that Japanese retain actual control in the status of 'advisers'?"

To this type of question, I can't help recalling the answer given by one of Ajinomoto's top executives when I traveled with him as a member of MITI's ASEAN Investment Climate Fact-Survey Mission a few years ago. He responded almost irritably — over sake on the rocks in private — "Why the hell do they ask this silly question over and over again? They seem to think that the production of glutamic acid is a very simple and foolproof process. But in actuality, we want to constantly update our operational efficiency and innovate methods to obtain better yields. To do this, we have to send out our engineers to teach newly developed know-how and effective production techniques. That's why we sometimes have to retain our expatriate advisers on the local scene for so long."

The JOEA (Japan Overseas Enterprise Association) model answer to this top question is based on their belief that Japanese-type management emphasizes human resources development. Their view is that people are of primary importance and that human resources constitute a company's most valuable assets, therefore human capability and potential always possess the possibility for broader development. The authors of the booklet insist that, quite rightly, instead of taking the attitude that "Well, if I just do this job that has been assigned to me, then that is the end of my responsibility," Japanese-type management stresses that each and every employee has an inherent ability for future growth. Thus, investment is made in the relationship with the capacity and potential of each employee. The Japanese expect "human growth" and "capability development" to be nurtured at the job site.

The last question is on desirable traits of the local managerial and supervisory staff. The question is: "What type of personality do Japanese look for in local managerial staff? Why is this so?"

The answer to this important question is very revealing of the true nature of Japanese managerial expectations. According to the book: "Local personnel at the managerial level in overseas Japanese companies appear to exhibit a certain personality profile which may be described as having the following characteristics:

    1. Motivation
    2. Honesty (in the sense of seriousness and honesty to one-self)
    3. Cooperativeness
    4. Patience

These four characteristics are significant because they are close to the virtues that Japanese personnel directors frequently emphasize in selecting ideal Japanese expatriates.

When we compare the Japanese descriptions with a typical American attempt to describe the IEBM (ideal expatriate businessman) as found in the brand-new *Americans Abroad — A Handbook for Living and Working Overseas* edited by J.Z. Kepler and others, we can identify striking similarities. The American version of the IEBM's attributes is as follows:

1. Patience
2. Sensitivity
3. Strength
4. Honesty
5. Team skills

Though these listed characteristics are not to be discussed in the same framework, they nevertheless suggest the validity of the recent emphasis on the commonality approach to management on both sides of the Pacific Basin.

How to Do Business in Japan (7)

Reading a Japanese like a Book Through the Body Language

Even the best-intentioned behavior of a visiting businessman from abroad sometimes gives us irritation and embarrassment, though we do not say so in public. One recent example to illustrate this was my encounter with a group of IBM engineers and executives. To my great surprise, all of them made very polite but abrupt one-hundred-degree bows in unison, saying *Hajimemashite, Yoroshiku* (How are you? I am very glad to see you.) They had apparently gone through the intensive cross-cultural orientation program to familiarize themselves with the Japanese language and culture. But Japanese, the 90-degree-or-more bow simply does not exist any longer, perhaps with the exception of a special audience with our Emperor.

When you are employed by a major Japanese department store, the first lesson you have to go through is how to differentiate your appropriate spine-bending practices, using a special device called "bowing angle meter." Their manuals suggest a forty-five-degree bow is sufficient to express a courteous welcome in your first encounter even with prestigious guest you have never met.

The very deep bow reminds us of the humiliating prewar kowtowing of the courtiers or low-ranking samurai who had to touch their forehead on the *tatami* mats when they were called by their lord.

Another example of behavior which makes the Japanese somewhat uneasy is to see a guest from overseas with their hands clasped in prayer when we meet them. It may be perfectly all right in meeting the Thais, or some Indians perhaps. We do not practice joining our hands with folded palms any longer in most of our social encounters, probably with some exceptions in the fundamentalist Buddhist believers and Ittoen religious group (a Japanese religious group which focuses upon humble and self-sacrificing devotion to humanity).

These are typical examples of our psychological discomfort in our contact with the well-intended mannerisms expressed by the visitors from abroad. But the foreign guests also experience uncomfortable Japanese body language and unconscious, nonverbal ways of expressing themselves.

The first and foremost behavior which often results in suspicion and misunderstanding is the Japanese lack of eye-contact in speaking to the foreigners. As a child, if a son looks straight into the eyes of his father when he is scolded, he might risks further angering the father. This is because obedience and piety is usually believed to be expressed by avoiding direct eye-contact and averting the eyes, while in most Western countries, keeping eye-contact is regarded as a sign of sincerity and honesty.

The second example of irritating body language to people from overseas is our pointing to a person with a forefinger, sometimes accompanied by quick shakes of that forefinger. This may be acceptable to politicians or orators who attempt to accuse their enemies in a non-Japanese environment. However, many Japanese businessmen, both young and old, perform this gesture quite unconsciously when they are with foreigners, let alone Japanese colleagues.

Speaking of forefinger movement, a common way to call an attention of the waiter in the United States is to keep your forefinger upright. But this may not necessarily work in the Japanese context. Sometimes this upward pointing with your forefinger remind the Japanese of a story of Great Buddha's birth in old India, when he stood immediately after the birth pointing to heaven with his right forefinger and pointing the earth with his left forefinger, saying "In the Heaven and on the Earth, I am not any man's man, but wholly my own." Therefore, if you want to get the attention of a waiter, you had better wave your hand or as Dr. Robert T. Moran, an expert on cross-cultural communication, suggests, "to extend the arm upward, palms down, and flutter forefingers." Moreover, knocking on the table may not work, but clapping your hands may be effective in a Japanese-style restaurant.

If you come from abroad for the first time to Japan, and bump into somebody, you might be upset because of the lack of "Excuse me" from the supposedly polite Japanese. Even though we try our best to keep an arm's length from others in congested traffic, most of us give up the idea of apologizing for unintentional physical contact with fellow Japanese citizens. For instance, in a day, the entire number of passengers getting on, getting off and going through the JNR Shinjuku station in Tokyo, is close to 2.5 million, which is almost equal to Singapore's population.

In most Western countries, scratching your heads, unless

you really feel itchy, is understood as a sign of not understanding what is being spoken. To the Japanese, scratching the head means that you are either trying to hide your clumsiness and embarrassment, or docile acceptance of your failure. Of course, to some Japanese, scratching can be interpreted as a sign of bewilderment and a perplexed state of mind. In some Western countries, formation of an "O" by making a circle with your thumb and forefinger is a gesture of either "OK" or "guaranteed." But if a Japanese makes this sign, it usually means money. But difference does not lie in cross-cultural meaning, but in actual position of the rest of the fingers when people make this sign. In a Western OK, the rest of the fingers are usually vertically extended and straight, while the other fingers in the Japanese gesture are slightly bent inwardly. If a Japanese waves his hands while forming this money sign horizontally, it means he has no money or he can not afford that much.

Professor Yuko Kobayashi, one of the foremost cross-cultural analysts of body codes, points out some subtle differences between Japanese and Western physical expression. For instance, sitting straight or in a rigid, upright position in Japan usually means he or she is seriously and formally ready to face an honorable guest or anybody who is superior in social ranking, while sitting in an upright position is normally a sign of surprise, shock or anxiety in the Western context.

In the Western world, sitting straight with legs crossed for a man is recommended as the most desirable way to express his confidence and composure. But, if you seat yourself with crossed legs in front of a Japanese, particularly a senior businessman, you will have a greater chance of being misunderstood as a rude, defiant, and aggressive person, because this gesture commonly suggests a provocation, a challenge and offensive attitude.

If you meet children and want to praise them, it is perfectly acceptable in Japan to pat and caress children on their heads, because this is a sign to signify a good child. But you'd better avoid this practice in most South-East Asian countries and some in Islamic countries, because the head is considered to be a sacred area where the spirit resides and should not be defiled by your touch. So when you are in Tokyo, at least try to do as Tokyoites are supposed to do.

How to Do Business in Japan (8)
Toward Better Understanding of Sogo Shosha

1984 is an important year for the U.S. marketeer, as it marks the actual launching of the American version of the sogo shosha (general trading firm) based on the Export Trading Act, which was recently passed to allow holding companies of U.S. banks to form export trading companies (ETCs) to compete with the powerful established traders of such nations as Japan, Great Britain, Hong Kong and Holland.

Therefore, a number of newly formed trading companies will be able to obtain approval from the U.S. government and will not be bothered by the stringent American anti-trust regulations when they do business overseas by banding together to handle larger shares of American products.

Sears, Roebuck & Co. and General Electric Co., together with Bank of America, Citibank, Security Pacific and First National Bank of Chicago plus some smaller regional firms are now awaiting the final decisions of the U.S. government before they start overall operations in overseas markets. This latest development to exploit the new law seems to have attracted resurgent attention to Japan's gigantic general trading companies, which are usually referred to as "sogo shosha." The sogo shosha have exerted a tremendous influence on Japan's pre- and postwar economic development. In fiscal 1982, some ¥17,857 billion in exports and ¥20,092 billion in imports, 63.3 percent and 92.4 percent of the nation's total, respectively, were managed by the top nine sogo shosha: Mitsubishi, Mitsui, C. Itoh, Marubeni, Sumitomo, Nissho Iwai, Toyo Menka, Kanematsu-Gosho and Nichimen.

Nevertheless, there are many aspects of the sogo shosha's extensive operations that are not fully appreciated by the overseas businessman.

The first area that is not always known to outsiders is the enormous range of products handled by the sogo shosha. It has been said jokingly that the sogo shosha sell everything from missiles to instant noodles, and this is not an exaggeration. Today, one recent favorite extension of their business activities is in the area of publishing. Even though this is not yet a full-fledged undertaking for the sogo shosha, Nissho Iwai's *Business Words Glossary* in seven languages and Mitsubishi's *Time Difference Is Money* were on the national non-fiction best-seller lists.

The second area that is not so familiar to non-Japanese businessmen is the fact that the sogo shosha are not merely merchants. They are major investors in both Japanese and overseas markets, with most joint venture companies in such regions as Malaysia, Indonesia and Singapore being jointly formed by the manufacturers and general trading firms. Another example of their investment operations is that the sogo shosha have been primarily responsible for major iron and steel distribution centers in Japan, which will cost more than ¥100 billion in total.

A third area involves the role of the sogo shosha as financier: the amount of money they use in a year usually reaches the level of 50 to 60 percent of the national budget. With such funds at their disposal, they can easily provide medium-term financing to a geat number of Japanese companies. In Japan, short-term financing is normally taken care of by ordinary banking institutions, long-term financing by government-related organizations. Thus, the sogo shosha are in a position to fill the needs of Japanese companies — particularly those that are internationally oriented in their dealings.

A fourth area is the dominance of the sogo shosha in the domestic sphere. A full 40.1 percent of the sogo shosha's business comes from their internal operations in the Japanese market.

A fifth aspect that is sometimes overlooked by the overseas analyst of the sogo shosha is their long history. Mitsui and Mitsubishi, for example, are both more than 100 years old.

One last area, which is gaining increasing momentum, is the sogo shosha's offshore trading activities. Cashing in on their huge international information networks, their business in connecting and integrating business interests in many parts of the world has contributed immensely to the success of so-called triangular offshore transactions. They not only buy and sell products, but make profits out of combining potential business opportunities abroad.

A sixth area that should not be forgotten in discussing the role of sogo shosha is their powerful assistance provided to plan contractors.

Because of their transactional expertise and thorough and extensive coverage of the many diversified industries, sogo shosha have undertaken a variety of development projects in all parts of the world. They are particularly strong in aiding the prospective

153

plant contractors in less developed regions. Here, their competence as system organizers is realized fully. Thus, *The Unique World of the Sogo Shosha,* compiled by Marubeni, confidently reports the advantages of working with sogo shosha on large-scale development projects: "their ability to organize a group of companies to carry out all aspects of large-scale projects, the stability of their overall activities and their high credit standing, their familiarity with overseas legal procedures and other requirements, their professional expertise in all aspects of international trade, and their ability to provide international marketing expertise which facilitates sale of the end products of these industrial projects."

In an effort to define the sogo shosha, Marubeni also mentioned their nature and functions as follows:

"Sogo shosha act as dealers in raw materials such as cotton and grain, just as international merchants do, but an important difference is the much wider line of raw materials handled by the sogo shosha and the overall size of their sales.

Sogo shosha differ from ordinary merchant trading houses in size, coverage of products, and international activities. Sogo shosha also differ from large retailing enterprises because they operate primarily at the wholesale level.

Another key role has been to coordinate and assist in the introduction of the latest technologies. Notably sogo shosha played an active role in mediating technology licensing arrangements, importing needed capital equipment, and providing other assistance for modernizing Japan's industries.

The sogo shosha, in summary, are unique business institutions combining many of the features of other businesses, including finance, but fundamentally oriented toward the task of facilitating trade flows and developing trade and industrial activity. The sogo shosha are trade specialists — experts in riding the tide of the world economy; highly flexible organizations capable of adjusting to the rise and fall of global demand."

Mr. Kyosuke Arita, an expert on the sogo shosha, describes these mammoth enterprises as excellent business organizers, brilliant systems integrators and conglomerate international merchants.

Thus, fledgling American trading firms may have to compete fiercely with the sogo shosha and their counterparts in other parts of the world from the very outset of operations.

How to Do Business in Japan (9)
Cashing In on the Changing Japanese Woman

A chance to make a profit always lies in change. In a tradition-bound society, opportunities to make money are generally quite limited but, in a drastically changing environment, even a fiddler on the roof, though his position may be shaky, can look around the old house and recognize a good oppotunity when he sees it — especially a business opportunity he can exploit. In this sense, the changing values and lifestyle of today's Japanese women are full of potential for those with imagination, courage and entrepreneurship.

If you go to Chiba Prefecture, adjacent to the Tokyo metropolitan area, you will find a good example of this. As a result of the careful examination of the changes taking places in the lives of Japanese housewives, a small, no-frills regional supermarket called Sanshi was established. Though open only from 9.00 a.m. to 1.00 p.m. daily, it is one of the most profitable of such operations in the area.

Why the strange store hours? Simply because the owner of the store discovered the easiest time for housewives to get things done is when their children are in school, between 9.00 a.m. and 1.00 p.m. And, fortunately, the sun shines brightest during those hours, providing free lighting for this energy-conscious, glass-roofed store.

The part-time housewives' only obligation as employees is to bring in one page of an old newspaper each morning they report for work at the store. Why a newspaper? So they have wrapping paper. This thrifty, publicity-shy store has made a greater profit than other food purveyors, for whom cut-throat competition is normal. Fifty-two percent of all housewives work and three-quarters of those without children, or who are free of the responsibility of caring for them, usually have a surplus four hours in which to find employment. If you can answer the question, "What kind of expenditure will immediately increase when your wife starts to work part-time?" you are set to benefit from the changing Japanese womens' demographics and psychographics. The right answers are (1) low-heeled shoes, (2) inexpensive pantyhose, (3) lipstick, and (4) extra money for going to coffee shops to chat.

Not long ago, I was able to interview two Japanese women who have recently become entrepreneurs and who have experienced instant success by focusing on and organizing Japanese womens' new interests.

Mrs. Yayoi Tsuda, only a licensed Japanese-language stenographer three years ago, is now the president of the rapidly-growing Yamato Professional Word Processing Center, which employs young, quickly-trained word-processing clerks. Major Japanese labor unions and local government offices are using Tsuda's fast transcription service. They can literally return to you the complete minutes of any conference within an hour and a half after the meeting adjourns. Most of the top prizes at the last national word-processing contest were won by her competent staff.

Another lady enjoying her newly created business is Mrs. Shigeko Shinohara, who literally " fell in love with computers." Less than four years after the inception of her idea, her Modern Information Research Institute is enjoying rapid growth and high profits. All her staffers are women, comprising students, housewives, divorcees, the young and the middle-aged. Some are pioneers, experimenting with the Japanese version of Alvin Tofler's cottage industry stay-at-home work style age.

When I asked why it is so profitable, Shinohara smilingly answered that her women executives never cheat on expenditure and in Japanese "M.C.P." society, most of the expense accounts are, fortunately, covered by businessmen full of false pride and dignity. Her firm was instrumental in designing Tokushima Prefecture's experimental project called Center for New Media and various other CAPTAIN-related projects. Her "I-hate-household-chores" program won the grand prix in last years Home Electonics Show.

These are the only two living testimonials to the successful tapping of both Japanese women's frustrations and ambitions for business purposes.

Several American-based or Japanese imitation psychological encounter training courses, which charge close to ¥150,000 ($640) for a five-day course designed to free participants of accumulated discontent and anxieties, are enjoying brisk growth. The training sessions are particularly popular among career-oriented women and nurses who are concerned that they are already beyond the socially accepted marriageable age.

The number of college-educated housewives who have

become franchisers, offering English conversation and math classes for children is burgeoning throughout Japan, as is the Tupperware-style home-party selling of lingerie, cosmetics and imported copper kitchenware.

A survey published recently by Hakuhodo Inc., a leading Japanese advertising agency, reveals that Japanese women commonly experience six basic phobia. While they feel confined by the mores of a society which down-plays the role of women, when they seek to take some degree of initiative contravening social dictates they enter a phase of self-doubt, which is reinforced by peer pressure. Then, at a loss regarding how to apply and adapt to their new-found role, they come to question its suitability and permanence.

Another interesting piece of market research carried out by the same agency last year probed the buying habits of Japanese housewives. Surprisingly, the Japanese housewife spent up to $20,000 a month on impulse purchases. The survey also disclosed, again surprisingly, that close to 70 percent of a typical housewife's purchases at a supermarket are not planned in advance. At department stores and supermarkets, over 70 percent of the candies, cookies and cakes are impulse purchases, while 54 percent of the sweaters, blouses and skirts for daily wear are bought spontaneously by housewives from their pocket money.

Many businessmen blame the five consecutive major snow storms this year in the Tokyo-Osaka megalopolis and do nothing about it. However, we should not overlook the three items which became bestsellers because of the heavy snow and the clever retailers who took advantage of the unexpected weather. First to sell out almost instantly were tire chains; second were chemically-activated hand-warming pouches, which likewise went very quickly; and, third, shovels and other items for removing snow.

Despite the substantial decrease in the disposable income of the average household during the past year, education-obsessed Japanese mothers spent 13.5 percent more on supplementary education for their children. Thus, the allocation of money for bringing up children remains the purview of Japanese mothers.

Vitamin drinks and pills, energizing snake-powder liquor, health drinks, jinseng and enzyme additives have all experienced a dramatic 26 percent increase in sales over last year.

How to Do Business in Japan (10)
The 'Time-Is-Short' Syndrome: Japan vs. the U.S.

Despite the numerous alleged differences between Americans and Japanese, there seems to be one thing they have in common on both sides of the Pacific Basin: The feeling that life is too short. That is why *The One Minute Manager,* by Kenneth Branchard and Spencer Johnson, which has sold close to one million copies in the U.S., has already enjoyed a Japanese readership of almost 300,000 in translation. Moreover, *The One Minute Father* and *The One Minute Mother,* by one of the authors of *The One Minute Manager,* were translated into Japanese only three months after publication and are read widely by frustrated mothers and fathers.

Putting The One Minute Manger at Work — the latest addition to the series — was published simulataneously in the U.S. and Japan early this month, the Japanese edition being a translation of the English. Fortunately, or unfortunetely, *The One Minute Lover,* a parody of *The One Minute Manager,* did

161

not attract enough attention to be put into Japanese, even though the work appears to have been given a wild reception and been widely read by hurried American businessmen.

Another humorous parody by two serious American Ph.Ds., titled *The 59 Seconds Employee,* is now being fought over by three Japanese publishers who seek to obtain the Japanese copyright.

The 59 Seconds Employee is designed to outsmart *The One Minute Manager* by preempting all managerial functions by one second. For instance, the writers of *The 59 Seconds Employee* suggest subordinates come up with their own, selfish objectives for presentation at one-minute, goal-setting meetings with the boss.

Even Mr. Edgar R. Fielder, economic researcher for the Conference Board, wrote a commentary "The One Minute Economist" in the February issue of "Across the Board" and, in Japan, there are already close to a dozen books with the words one minute in the title.

On this side of the Pacific, *The One Minute Manager* is particularly favored by managers of chain stores, fast-food chains, banks and other financial institutions, as well as of the large, traditional organizations. This series of books has generated enormous interest among business people because of the magic of the title and its subsequent appeal to time-hungry businessmen and organizers. While they are fully aware that "there is very little worth doing what can be done in a minute," those caught up in the rat race will grasp any quick fix.

In the U.S., where 53 percent of the women aged over 16 are in the labor market and the majority of them are involved in professional work, the feeling that time is short is keenly felt by working women. This is particularly true of working mothers, who desire not only to perform their jobs satisfactorily, but simultaneously to be good housewives, excellent mothers and wonderful wives. That is why one can find dozens of guidebooks designed to help working women better organize their time.

In this area, Japan is still about 15 to 20 years behind the U.S. It is only recently that Japanese housewives have started to work part-time and so there are not as many books in Japan dedicated to the more efficient carrying out of household chores as in the U.S.

While Westerners might say "Time flies like a jet," Japanese will quote the old Chinese saying "Time flies like an arrow." When Bernard Berensen says, "I would I could stand on a busy corner, hat in hand, and beg people to throw me all their wasted hours," Japanese businessmen will sympathize with the traditional Japanese saying, "Enjoy an interval of leisure snatched from busy life." And though Japanese executives will often start their conversation with the stereotype greeting, "Oisogashii desuka?" (Are you busy?), most of them do not believe that being busy is something of which to be proud but, rather, a disgrace to the gentleman, as an English proverb states.

If you think that Tokyo is the busiest city in Japan, you are wrong. According to one interesting study by a Japanese sociologist, the walking speed of Osaka pedestrians in the morning rush hour is slightly faster than that of Tokyoites. One of the agonies frequently voiced by travelling business people of late is that, since bullet trains now connect Tokyo with other major cities, they have been robbed of the joys of staying overnight in localities where there is less hustle and bustle as they can — and so must — return to Tokyo on the same day.

The obsession with punctuality may be another problem shared by most of today's business executives in Japan. Whereas a meeting will usually start from thirty to forty minutes late in Brazil and perhaps ten minutes late in the U.S., it gets under way on time in Japan — much like the punctuality-obsessed Japanese National Railway. We know, as Prof. Peter F. Drucker advocates, time is now the most important of business-related resources, which cannot be replenished in spite of the increased demand for it. Nevertheless, we seem to have more respect for what is sacrificed by the busy, ultra-time conscious American businessman — warm, interpersonal relations, quality of goods, services and working lives, and aesthetic values.

That is why tele-conferences and TV telephone networks are far less developed and used than previously anticipated, though the systems are technically feasible. If you happen to meet an old-style Japanese businessman, you may sometimes be baffled by his very strong insistence on personally seeing you, although the matter could easily be dealt with by phone or telex.

Having said all this, I have to hasten to add that the younger Japanese people are more accepting of a faster business pace and they enjoy a speedier exchange of information and ideas, as can be observed from the many TV and radio programs for the young. It might be interesting to add that the Japanese word *toki* (time) is derived from *tokeru,* which means to melt away.

There is a great potential for those shrewd marketers who tap the need felt by young people in Japan for faster service to save time. You can, for example, sell them a beeper to signal that the bathtub is full to the brim and you can cash in big by marketing a simple hour glass for the Kyoto Royal Hotel coffee shop where it is served guests together with their pot of tea. When the sand has sifted through to the bottom of the hour glass, in exactly three minutes, the customer knows the tea is just right for drinking.

One Japanese journalist who heard why President Reagan did not suffer from jet lag on his last visit to Japan learned of the existence of the U.S. Department of Energy program called The Argonne Anti-Jet-Lag Diet and is now busily engaged in adopting the reportedly most effective formula to avoid jet lag through the Feast-East-Feast-Fast system.

But, despite all the efforts to conquer time, the age-old quotes, "Time goes, you say? Ah no! Time says, we go," and "Time is a great healer, but a very poor beautician," will stay with us as never-changing truths.